Black Eye
for America

Praise for *Black Eye for America*

"Carol Swain and Christopher Schorr have written the first truly comprehensive and lucid book describing the essence, history, and true intentions of critical theory. They explain the origins of critical race theory and its relationship to current politics, history, civil rights, and traditional American values. They end by offering effective strategies for challenging and resisting it. Unlike most descriptions of critical theory that leave one simply with a new set of confusing words, e.g., Marxism, here all things are explained in cogent language with clear examples. I have taught critical theory in graduate classes for twenty years and this is the most accessible and thorough explanation of its tenets, historical effects, and its real intentions around the world. If you wondered if you would ever see an accessible explanation regarding critical theory or critical race theory, the search is over—Swain and Schorr have pulled it all together here."

— **Mary Poplin**, professor, Claremont Graduate University

"Critical race theory is attempting to revive racial prejudice, perverting justice and using discrimination as a social weapon. Carol Swain and Christopher Schorr's book is exactly what Americans need to understand the threat critical race theory poses to all of us—and to help individuals, families, and communities chart a course to the American Dream."

— **Jonathan Butcher,** Institute for Family, Community, and Opportunity, and The Heritage Foundation

"To fight evil ideas, a society needs people with intelligence and courage. Without the latter, civilization as we know it will simply disintegrate. That is why *Black Eye for America* is so important: the authors combine equal amounts of intelligence and courage. If you want to understand Critical Race Theory and, most importantly, why it is the antithesis of every beautiful idea in the American and Western worlds, read this book."

— **Dennis Prager,** nationally syndicated talk show host, founder of the internet-based Prager University, and a *New York Times* bestselling author.

Black Eye
for America

HOW CRITICAL RACE THEORY IS
BURNING DOWN THE HOUSE

Carol M. Swain PhD &
Christopher J. Schorr PhD

Copyright©2021 by Carol M. Swain and Christopher J. Schorr
All rights reserved. Written permission must be secured from the publisher or
the authors to use or reproduce any part of this book, except for brief quotations in
critical reviews or articles.

ISBN: 978-1-7374198-0-8

Cover design by 360 Media Group.
Cover photo of burning flag provided by Natanael Ginting.
Author back cover photos by Bearashkin Inc., P.O. Box 1102, Rockville, MD 20849.

Copies of *Black Eye for America* can be ordered in bulk through Logos Books,
logosnashville@gmail.com

Printed in the United States of America

To my past, present, and future students who deserve a better world than the one we are creating through humanism and to the Americans who decried what has happened to America

— Carol M. Swain

To Ibram X. Kendi, whose work provides so much fodder for this book

— Chris Schorr

"Everything Is Beautiful"

Jesus loves the little children
All the children of the world
Red and yellow, black and white
They are precious in His sight
Jesus loves the little children of the world

Everything is beautiful in its own way
Like a starry summer night or a snow-covered winter's day
And everybody's beautiful in their own way
Under God's Heaven the world's gonna find a way

There is none so blind
As he who will not see
We must not close our minds
We must let our thoughts be free
For every hour that passes by
You know the world gets a little bit older
It's time to realize that beauty lies
In the eyes of the beholder

And everything is beautiful
In its own way
Like a starry summer night or a snow-covered winter's day
And everybody's beautiful in their own way
Under God's Heaven
The world's gonna find a way

We shouldn't care about the length of his hair
Or the color of his skin
Don't worry about what shows from without
But the love that lives within
We're gonna get it all together now
Everything's gonna work out fine
Just take a little time
Look on the good side my friend
Straighten it out in your mind

("Everything Is Beautiful,"
reprinted with permission by Ray Stevens, Ahab Music.)

"From one man he made all the nations, that they should inhabit the whole earth; and he marked out their appointed times in history and the boundaries of their lands." Acts 17:26

Contents

Foreword

HISTORY IS FULL OF HINGE MOMENTS; THOSE TIMES WHEN SOMEONE CHOOSING to act or not act, or an event going this way or that, have profound consequences. Take George Washington's short circuiting the Newburgh Conspiracy; John Adams's choosing to peacefully hand control of the executive branch to his ideological opponent; Abraham Lincoln's fighting to keep the southern states in the Union; or the American people's choosing to support Ronald Reagan's efforts to smash the Soviet Union and its Communist aims. In each of these situations, the outcome was not preordained; had things turned out differently, the world likely would be a much worse place.

We are at a similar hinge point today. Our country is fractured and in danger of coming apart at the seams. The misguided ideology of Critical Race Theory is corrupting our institutions, dividing Americans by race, and pitting them against one another based on that arbitrary characteristic. So, the American people are faced with a choice: do the better angels of our nature unite and guide the country back toward the ideals of the Declaration of Independence, that all men are created equal and endowed by their Creator with certain unalienable rights? Or do we succumb to the forces of darkness and division, which will lead to further social conflict in a nation that cannot afford to be any more divided?

There is only one just outcome in this fight. Our only option is to treat people as individuals, with their race being only one characteristic of the complex web of traits that makes up who they are, and an unimportant one at that. But Critical Race Theory does not allow this; in fact, it requires the opposite. For Critical Race Theory, the only characteristic that matters is a person's race. And individuals are not individuals, but members of racial groups who are only judged collectively as a racial group. Any differences between racial groups are exclusively the result of racism, as opposed to any other factor.

But just because there is only one just outcome does not mean that outcome will prevail. While the premises of Critical Race Theory are self-evidently false, both in theory and in fact, Critical Race Theory remains on the march. Its advocates are gaining strength, indoctrinating our children, and infiltrating institutions at an alarming rate. The forces fighting for the just outcome are on the defensive.

This book and its authors are needed allies in this battle. *Black Eye for America* clearly and cogently explains how and why the embrace of Critical Race Theory will bankrupt our nation both spiritually and intellectually. The authors dissect the purported intellectual framework of Critical Race Theory, exposing it for what it is: a warmed-over Marxism that substitutes race for class but otherwise embraces the same failed ideas and assumptions of an ideology that sent 100 million people to their graves. The book also explains how Critical Race Theory is anti-American, anti-liberal in the classical sense, and anathema to the Judeo-Christian values that are the bedrock of the American ethos.

While neo-Marxist in theory, Critical Race Theory is neo-Jim Crow in practice, having simply swapped which race is favored and which race is disfavored. The book provides a helpful road map for countering the creep of Critical Race Theory and its pernicious influence. It outlines strategies and tactics to fight back, from how to channel the idea of insurgency to achieve much-needed reforms to how to exit institutions that cannot be fixed.

Dr. Swain and Dr. Schorr have done the world, and Americans in particular, a great service by writing this book. I look forward to people of good faith using the arguments within it to fight against the forces of destruction and bring our country back into the light.

— **Dr. Benjamin Carson**
Chairman and founder of the American Cornerstone Institute

Acknowledgments

I WOULD LIKE TO THANK THE PEOPLE ACROSS THE NATION WHO URGED ME TO write a book explaining Critical Race Theory and what we can do about it. Given that there are only 24 hours in a day and 168 hours in a week, what seemed impossible in the beginning has been achieved. God gave me the strength and determination to start the project, and he brought Chris Schorr into my life. What started off as a research assistantship gradually evolved into a co-authorship. Chris's passion for this project, and his intellect and knowledge of American history, academia, and political science proved invaluable.

Jaymee Westover, a summa cum laude Vanderbilt University graduate, has worked with me since she was an undergraduate. She worked tirelessly on our manuscript and made substantive contributions. Jaymee is one of those amazing young women who does outstanding work while balancing the needs and demands of a growing family. Mike Towle, a long-time friend and editor, suggested the title, edited the manuscript, and guided it through the publication process. I am especially grateful for those who pray for me daily: to my sons Benjamin and Reginald; my five grandchildren, Destiny, Storm, Skye, Tiera, and Chelsea; my great-grandson Hezekiah; and my good friend Donna Willis, who serves as a sounding board. A shoutout to Olivia Lan, who will one day write her own book.

Lastly, I would like to thank my ninety-one-year-old mother Dorothy and her caregiver, Gwen, for their patience and understanding of the schedule I keep and the life I live.

— Carol

This project came together in a short period of time and grew well beyond its initial, more-limited scope. I am deeply grateful to everyone who helped to make this possible, beginning with Carol Swain for asking me to partner with her on this exciting, timely, and important project. I am grateful as well for Jaymee Westover's dedication and excellent research work. Finally, I am grateful to my wife Aja, as always, for her patience.

— Chris

Black Eye
for America

CHAPTER 1

Introduction

WHY WE CAME TOGETHER TO WRITE THIS BOOK

I (CAROL) AM A FORMER UNIVERSITY PROFESSOR WHO FOR MANY YEARS HAS BEEN warning people about Critical Race Theory and its impact on our society. As a professor of both political science and law, I have watched CRT metastasize like a cancer on college and university campuses. Alongside political correctness—another blight on civil discourse—CRT has stoked racial turmoil and helped to spawn cancel culture, safe spaces, trigger warnings, racially segregated dorms and graduations, and, on some campuses, separate course sections by race. Universities are no longer the marketplaces of ideas they once were. I fear for my country now that CRT has migrated from college campuses to society-at-large.

In 2017, I took early retirement and left the university environment to focus my time and energy on issues that would impact a larger public. As an author, public speaker, political commentator, and entrepreneur, I dedicate my time to reaching and equipping people with the information they need to fight back against the creeping rot destroying our nation. As I frequently tell people, the world is my classroom. From the media platform I have been given, I sound an alarm when I see danger and deception in American political and religious life. I am writing this book precisely for this purpose.

I am deeply troubled by changes that are reversing gains our nation has made in the areas of civil rights and equal opportunity. My concern for

America coupled with my visibility as a scholar and as a public intellectual from humble beginnings led me to join forces with Bob Woodson of the Woodson Center. Woodson formed 1776 Unites[1] in fall 2019 after *The New York Times* launched its controversial *1619 Project,* which made false, sweeping claims about slavery and America's founding.[2] Our united efforts led to the 2021 publication of *Red, White, and Black: Rescuing American History from Revisionists and Race Hustlers.*[3] In December of 2020, President Donald Trump appointed me to a two-year term as vice-chair of the 1776 Commission. Our charge was to write a report on "core principles of the American founding and how these principles might be used to teach patriotism and civics in preparation for the 250th anniversary of the Declaration of Independence." Our committee met twice before it was dissolved by Trump's successor, President Joe Biden, on Inauguration Day as one of his first acts in office. I am pleased to report that the 1776 Commission is still active. We reconvened in May 2021 to develop a strategy to respond to Critical Race Theory and how it is impacting our nation.

Dr. James Lindsay, co-author of *Cynical Theories: How Activist Scholarship Made Everything about Race, Gender, and Identity—And Why This Harms Everybody*[4] defines Critical Race Theory as the "belief that racism is the organizing principle of society."[5] Lindsay and Helen Pluckrose's timely analysis traces the evolution of the dangerous ideologies ripping our nation apart. We have now reached a point in America where racism with a Marxist twist is state-sanctioned and enforced by our major social institutions. Indeed, our public and private K-12 schools are ground zero in the battle. White children are taught to be ashamed of their skin color on the grounds that they unjustly benefit from a "white supremacist" system established by their ancestors to oppress racial and ethnic minorities. Black children are taught that they are victims of a thoroughly (and permanently) racist system. American children of all races are taught that they live in an evil nation that has wreaked great harm on the world.

In December 2019, I was approached by a group of parents of Christian students enrolled in Lipscomb Academy, a private Church of Christ-affiliated institution in Nashville, Tennessee. Lipscomb Academy operates under the auspices of Lipscomb University and was formed by its board of trustees. These parents were troubled by the lower school's decision to hire a dean of intercultural development. The young black woman hired described herself as a "radical liberator, educator, minister, and organizer." An activist's activist, one of her first acts was to create a black student union. Until this action, the school did not have a history of separating students by race. Parents were rightly concerned that this newly hired dean was an active supporter of Black Lives Matter and had a personal website with statements condemning white people and Church of Christ doctrine on the role of women in the church. I wrote three essays addressing this issue: "Does Progress Require Shaming and Embarrassing Our Children?" "Critical Race Theory and Christian Education," and "Critical Race Theory Is Rooted in Cultural Marxism."[6] Several of the school's administrators left their positions, but Critical Race Theory continues to influence Lipscomb University. In spring 2021, prominent critical race theorist Dr. Ibram X. Kendi was featured as the premier speaker at a Christian Scholars Conference at Lipscomb University.[7] When this information was revealed, the first impulse of the University was to hide it by removing the announcement from its website. Lipscomb later reinstated the advertisement after a conservative newspaper revealed their actions.[8]

Using a racist ideology that masquerades as "antiracism" to divide Americans by skin color is repugnant. Every parent should watch shaming videos such as "Your Brain on Drug Policy"[9] and "The Unequal Opportunity Race"[10] to better understand what is happening in our children's schools. Shockingly, these videos are shown to middle school and high school-aged children: kids ill-equipped to handle heavy-duty messaging about racism and collective guilt. In some schools, the new quest for "equity" in place of equal opportunity and colorblindness is resulting in the removal of advanced placement courses and other opportunities for gifted children. There is also a move to *force* equity by removing entrance exams and testing for admission to elite schools.

A corollary to Critical Race Theory is Intersectionality. This is a theory asserting that overlapping sources of oppression compound one another, rendering racial and ethnic minorities, gays and lesbians, and economically disadvantaged groups *even more* marginalized and victimized by society in proportion to their accumulating victim identities.[11] Intersectionality advocates claim that the lived experiences of more marginalized people carry more weight than those of less-marginalized people; indeed, marginalized people's experiences are claimed to carry more weight than empirical evidence.

In writing this book, I have teamed up with Dr. Chris Schorr, a young man who as a student discovered me and worked to quantify some of the ideas in my 2002 book, *The New White Nationalism in America: Its Challenge to Integration.*[12] In *Black Eye for America*, we hope to make it easier for people to understand what is happening and how they can more effectively resist what we consider to be a dangerous and evil agenda that rises to the level of a civil rights threat. This is the time, we contend, for people of all races and ethnicities to lock arms to fight against this worldview—one that is destroying healthy race relations and making it more difficult for minorities to build upon successes they achieved in previous generations. Critical Race Theory now permeates our churches, military, and intelligence agencies, as well as our institutions of higher learning and even K-12. It needs to be stopped in its tracks by knowledgeable people imbued with courage and the lofty principles that made America the envy of the free world.

CHRISTOPHER J. SCHORR'S PERSPECTIVE

I recently came to this topic as part of my dissertation research addressing the threat posed by white nationalism to conservative politics in the United States.[13] That research led me first to Dr. Carol Swain's definitive work on white nationalism[14] and then, fortunately, to Carol herself. From an academic standpoint, I was intrigued by the political implications of rising white identification and white consciousness. For a variety of reasons, racial identity has been less salient for whites in America than for members of other groups; however, recent research demonstrates that this is beginning to change.[15] As a personal matter, I was (and remain) deeply concerned as to the effects of racial identity politics on our nation's integrity. Being a US Marine (there are no "ex-Marines"), I take these things personally.

The role of public discourse was among the several factors I considered as possible contributors to rising white identification. A recent torrent of condemnation of white people and of white identity in popular media, along with equivalent, if not *greater,* condemnations of American society as "white supremacist" and "systemically racist" caught my attention. Presumably, I thought, whites had taken notice. Such rhetoric had been imported into American media and culture from formerly obscure, radical academic fields of study such as Critical Race Theory, Whiteness Studies, and from related "cultural Marxist" "studies" fields.

Like most Americans, I was both aware and generally contemptuous of political correctness and of identity politics; however, it was clear that this

CRT phenomenon was something else entirely. CRT is far from "antiracism," the term adopted by its proponents. It is, rather, *explicitly racist*, demeaning designated "oppressor" and "oppressed" groups alike. CRT condemns people in the former category for the alleged sins of their birth, compelling them, in practice, to humiliate themselves in absurd, ritualistic fashions. CRT infantilizes and denigrates people in the latter category, describing them as hapless victims of a society that belongs to someone else. Previous (i.e., authentic) champions of racial equality fought to incorporate people of color into the story of America—perhaps, the *second-greatest* story ever told. CRT inverts that story by declaring exceptions to the rule—cases where America failed to live up to its founding and purpose—to be the rule itself (see the *1619 Project*). In so doing, CRT degrades the object toward which advocates of racial justice strove and, especially in regard to people of color, it diminishes the value of American citizenship.

It is my (and our) sincere hope that this book helps to inform readers of CRT's pernicious influence. Most importantly, we hope to mobilize readers to resist and defeat CRT wherever they find it: in politics, in workplaces, in schools (especially in *children's* schools), in churches, and everywhere else it rears its ugly head.

WHERE WE STAND

We want to be clear upfront about our stance. We acknowledge the nation's tragic racial past and the strides that have been made to create a more just society. Women, as well as racial and ethnic minorities, have benefitted from efforts to address and correct for past and present discrimination. Our civil rights laws and affirmative action as law and policy were part of our nation's efforts to create opportunities and a just society. What is happening today goes far beyond any of the inequities associated with the preferential policies associated with affirmative action.

We both are devout Christians who believe God created one human race and that the distinctions we see are man-made. We acknowledge that racism and prejudice are sinful acts that are always wrong and should always be condemned regardless of the race or ethnicity of the perpetrator. In making this statement, we reject arguments made by critical race theorists and other leftists who falsely claim that only whites can be racists. According to this narrative, being born into the white race automatically makes one a blood-guilty white supremacist in possession of ill-gotten gains derived from racial oppression.

We also reject the bullying and shaming of white people just as all decent people reject such acts of racism against blacks, Hispanics, Asians, and Native Americans. Whether it is against whites or blacks, racial discrimination is counter to who we are as Americans, and it violates state and federal civil rights laws as well as the principles enshrined in the Fourteenth Amendment's Equal Protection Clause. We are staunchly opposed to political activism and indoctrination disguised as education and to so-called "antiracism" programs and training that, in reality, use racism as an attempted remedy for racial and ethnic disparities.

THE PATH FORWARD

Our book is divided into eight chapters. In this first chapter, we have addressed why we believe that this book is now urgently needed. In chapter 2, we address how, in theory and in practice, Critical Race Theory (CRT) divides Americans and pits them against each other and against their own country. Chapter 3 explains CRT's historical and scholarly background. In chapters 4 and 5, we argue that CRT is irreconcilable with traditional American principles; specifically, with America's classical liberal (chapter 4) and Christian (chapter 5) inheritance. Most importantly, in chapter 6, we argue that CRT is inconsistent with the U.S. Constitution's Equal Protection Clause and, depending on how it is implemented, that it can violate the Civil Rights Act of 1964 and the education amendments added to it in 1972. CRT additionally often compels speech and action contrary to First Amendment protections. In chapter 7, we account for CRT's rapid spread through the major institutions of American society and develop several "big picture" strategies for resisting its pernicious effects. We conclude in chapter 8 with ten specific proposals, including policies that need your support as well as actions you can take to personally combat CRT.

Our targeted audiences for this book are anyone affected (or who will be affected) by the spread of CRT. These include:

- Children, parents with school-aged children (including college students), and people who care about opportunities for children
- Working adults

- Religious observers and anyone concerned with religious liberty
- Social media users and anyone concerned with freedom of expression
- People who consume media and culture
- Patriotic Americans who believe in the principles of *e pluribus unum* (out of many, one), and
- People who believe that truth exists and that there is an objective, real world.

If you fall into one or more of these categories, this book is written for you.

CHAPTER 2

What Is
Critical Race Theory?

CRITICAL RACE THEORY IS A FUNDAMENTALLY RACIST WORLDVIEW PREDICATED on the claim that racism is in the "DNA" of American institutions and society, as well as, in effect, in the DNA of white Americans. It sees minorities, especially black Americans, as victims of "systemic racism": racism permeating a vast network of impenetrable institutional structures and cultural stereotypes—all created by whites to give themselves unearned advantages. This depressing narrative states that government-sponsored racism did not end in the 1960s when Congress passed three major civil rights bills to address the effects of Jim Crow racism. Evidently, nothing of real consequence took place following the passage of the Civil Rights Act of 1964, which mandated the advertising of jobs and banned discrimination based on race, color, sex, religion, or national origin. Likewise, the Voting Rights Act of 1965 and the Open Housing Act of 1968 did little to deinstitutionalize racial discrimination in American law and society.

In reality, the civil rights laws of this era ended "institutional racism"—racism sanctioned by the government—by law, creating equal opportunities for millions of women and for racial minorities. The racism that remained "in the system" was individual in nature. Laws cannot strike prejudice from people's hearts; however, here too, great progress has been made. In 1958, only 4 percent of Americans approved of marriages between blacks and whites; by 2013, approval of interracial marriage had risen to 87 percent across the board and to 84 percent among whites.[1] Today, Americans report far greater political than racial animosity.[2] The success of millions of racial and ethnic minorities, and the election and re-election of a black president (Barack Obama), are testament to America's great racial progress. Racism in America has been overwhelmingly *de*-systematized; however, Critical Race Theory now threatens to undo this great work and to drag our country backward towards racial antipathy and separation.

CRT proponents have jettisoned the quest for racial reconciliation and a colorblind society where individuals are free to pursue their dreams for a better life. In place of equal opportunity, CRT demands equity—equal *outcomes* by group. To this end, CRT demands discrimination in favor of some groups and against others. In practice, CRT advocates often demand more than equity (i.e., permanent advantages) for so-called "victims" as they work to turn the tables on "oppressors."

CRT targets white people, singling out a racial group for mistreatment. This blatant racial discrimination makes CRT the greatest civil rights issue of our time. CRT proponents justify racial discrimination (on *their* terms) by claiming that whites derive tremendous unearned advantages from the color of their skin. Whites, they claim, possess vested "property interests" in their "whiteness," which they must divest themselves of in pursuit of equity and to shed their (innate and inherited) racial guilt. This process (becoming "antiracist") entails confessing complicity in racism and challenging other whites who likewise benefit from the institutional structures that allegedly perpetuate "white supremacy."

White people who claim to be innocent of the charge of racism and discrimination are deemed guilty of harboring *hidden* racial biases. It does not matter if the white person is a descendant of abolitionists, including those who risked their lives sheltering runaway slaves in the underground railroad, or if he/she hails from a philanthropic family that gave millions of dollars to set up black schools and universities. White people are "oppressors" by definition. Christianity, and Western civilization more broadly, also falls into the oppressor category.

On the other hand, racial and ethnic minorities, especially black people, are described as helpless victims in need of liberation from pervasive and persistent systemic racism. This patronizing account strips minorities of ownership and control over their own lives while attributing to whites seemingly godlike powers to create every sort of malady in black homes and communities. CRT thus harms its intended beneficiaries by creating a sense of hopelessness while eroding decades of goodwill—in some cases, goodwill painstakingly built—between members of different racial and ethnic groups.

The narratives and "lived experiences" of blacks and other "oppressed" groups are elevated to a morally superior position over facts, science, and historical data that run counter to its core claims. Every minority is qualified to critique and re-educate others about systemic harms. A failure to agree with a proponent of CRT demands re-education rather than honest debate. Such "struggle sessions" harken back to CRT's Marxist origins (more on this to come).

One of our points of emphasis concerns the spread of CRT throughout the educational arena. In K-12 schools, in particular, CRT rarely presents itself as "CRT"; rather, it hides behind euphemistic labels such as "antiracism," "educational equity," and "cultural competency." Such methods are plainly deceitful. CRT advocates market themselves as engaged in a noble effort to combat systemic racism and to bring about a just and fair distribution of resources, in the process rooting out pernicious explicit or implicit—i.e., conscious or unconscious—racial biases. In practice, however, such instruction distorts American history to manufacture conclusions that would never hold up in an honest debate where both sides were able to marshal evidence.

Under CRT-inspired instruction in K-12 schools, American children are now taught to view racism as the cornerstone of American society. They are taught that whites dominate a racial hierarchy in America and exercise power *as a group*. White students (again, children) are forced to confront their supposed "hidden racism" and its effect on society. In some school districts, claims of systemic racism are introduced to students in the first grade. By junior high, students are taught radical and divisive perspectives on "whiteness"— e.g., that any white person who has failed to proclaim himself or herself an "antiracist" is a "white supremacist," regardless of whether he or she rejects notions of racial superiority. Much like employees undergoing "diversity, equity, and inclusion" training, students are strongly discouraged from challenging these claims and have been punished for doing so.[3] There's more.

Concepts such as colorblindness, assimilation, and merit are dismissed as cynical means by which whites maintain their power and privilege in American society. The great achievements of the civil rights movement are consequently disparaged, as are the achievements of black people who were not victims and who refused to see themselves as such. How this distorted vision of racial oppression will benefit American society, much less the children exposed to it, is anyone's guess. Will white children benefit from the self-loathing imparted to them by CRT instructors? Or from the bullying, shaming, intimidation, and hostility they experience as a result of it? Will black and other minority children benefit from instruction aimed at eviscerating their personal agency—their sense of being in control of their own lives, rather than being at the mercy of mercurial (systemic) forces?

At this point, many readers of this book will ask themselves where this hateful and divisive ideology comes from. To answer that question, we first turn to two prominent CRT proponents, husband and wife Richard Delgado and Jean Stefancic, both of whom are law professors and social critics. Delgado, believed to be one of the founders of CRT, and Stefancic define CRT as, "a collection of activists and scholars interested in studying and transforming the relationship among race, racism, and power."[4] Studying race, racism, and power seems like a worthy pursuit, unlike say, bullying children. How then might the one lead to the other? How is it that CRT scholars and activists go about their task?

In simple terms, CRT views American society and government through a Marxist analytical lens, emphasizing group power and group conflict. Readers might be familiar with the standard Marxist worldview wherein the social order is defined by the oppression of workers (the "proletariat") by the capitalist classes (the "bourgeoisie"). From this vantage point, social institutions—economic, social, security, religious, cultural, etc.—are all described as elements of capitalist oppression. Marxists consequently advocate upending the social order and reconstituting society along socialist lines.

In CRT and in related fields (more on this later), racial and other social categories substitute for economic classes. White people (but also, men, heterosexuals, and Christians) are thus defined as "oppressors" and people of color (but also, women, gays, and religious minorities) are defined as "oppressed." Given that, again, per Marxism, society and government are understood in terms of the domination of oppressed groups by oppressor groups, CRT treats racism as "the organizing principle of society."[5] Like their ideological forebearers, CRT proponents aim to overthrow the social order on behalf of the "oppressed."

In this context, terms such as "white supremacy" and "institutional racism" are not restricted to historic systems such as Jim Crow or apartheid but are used to describe contemporary Western, and especially American, society. CRT asserts that slavery and racial segregation were never contrary to American values; instead, America was always and remains a white supremacist wolf cloaked in a universalistic, (classical) liberal sheep's clothing. Core American values such as individualism, liberty, meritocracy, property rights, and even procedural equality are viewed as expressions of white supremacy and/or fig leaves to obscure white supremacy from public view.

CRT proponents make expansive and exaggerated claims about racism in America. They find racism nearly everywhere, including in day-to-day interactions where the uninitiated might never think to look—e.g., a stranger failing to wave to you.[6] In this view, racism is the primary cause for differences in outcomes between racial groups—e.g., in income, educational attainment, incarceration etc. It cannot be the case, for example, that a black/white difference in incarceration rates could exist independent of *present-day* racial oppression. For example, to the CRT advocate, pointing out that violent crime rates differ by racial group,[7] and that violent crime presumably has something to do with incarceration, misses the point. All disparities reflect unequal (racist) treatment *somewhere* in "the system."

This perspective is perhaps most prominently advanced by Ibram X. Kendi. Kendi explains, "When I see racial disparities, I see racism. But I know for many racist Americans, when they see racial disparities, they see black inferiority."[8] He thus treats racial disparities (unequal outcomes) as straight-forward evidence of racial discrimination (unequal treatment). The system must be racist, Kendi argues, because absent racial discrimination, the only explanation for racial disparities must be that some racial groups are just *better* than others—e.g., smarter, less criminally inclined, etc. This is a simplistic and disingenuous argument.

In reality, group disparities are commonplace and do not always[9] favor so-called "dominant groups." Moreover, there is a world of difference between saying "X group is doing better/worse in some respect than Y group" and saying, "X group is superior to Y group." A given disparity between groups (however defined) may have any number of causes. It isn't obvious, for example, that the gender incarceration disparity[10] reflects systemic, matriarchal oppression (institutional misandry). Likewise, the fact that Asian Americans earn more on average[11] than white Americans isn't obviously a product of white (or Asian) supremacy.

Racial discrimination exists, including "old-fashioned" discrimination against racial minorities (the kind CRT opposes), but, to support a claim of racial discrimination, one needs *evidence* of racial discrimination. Disparate group outcomes simply aren't that. Understanding this fact alone goes a long way toward countering a great many claims of systemic racism. Not to worry, though. CRT has plenty of other "racisms" to consider.

Perhaps the most remarkable of these is "colorblind racism." In layman's terms, "colorblind racism" is the "racism" embodied in Dr. Martin Luther King' Jr.'s "I Have a Dream" speech. It is the "racism" of attempting to view people primarily as members of some shared supraordinate category—as Americans, human beings, children of God, etc.—rather than primarily as members of racial groups ("color consciousness").

If that description sounds implausible, consider the following from a *Psychology Today* article titled "Colorblind Ideology Is a Form of Racism."[12] The article correctly describes colorblindness as an "ideology that posits the best way to end discrimination is by treating individuals as equally as possible, without regard to race, culture, or ethnicity." It then acknowledges that colorblindness amounts to "really taking MLK seriously on his call to judge people on the content of their character rather than the color of their skin. It focuses on commonalities between people, such as their shared humanity." The article then goes on to explain why ignoring skin color is racist.

In short, the CRT argument against colorblindness is an extension of the systemic racism concept.[13] Colorblindness, like individualism and meritocracy, is said to obscure structures of racial oppression, allowing whites to continue to dominate people of color. CRT offers other noteworthy "racisms" (e.g., "new," "cultural," and "aversive" racisms) and related concepts (e.g., cultural appropriation);[14] however, the most important remaining concept is the revision CRT makes to ordinary or unqualified "racism." This revision is commonly referred to as the "prejudice plus power" definition of racism, which claims that only white people can be racist.[15] The argument promotes the idea that only dominant group members possess the "institutional power" to link racial prejudice to meaningful action—i.e., to do racist things. White people's racial prejudices ("racism") thus carry extra weight compared to that of racial prejudices held by people of color (not "racism").

In practice, this theory means that statements such as the following from Nation of Islam leader Louis Farrakhan are "not racist": "White people deserve to die, and they know, so they think it's us coming to do it."[16] Such a statement would be called "racist" if uttered by a white speaker substituting the word "white" for "black." Hypocrisy is one of the hallmarks of CRT. It is also noteworthy that the prejudice plus power definition does not take into account power differences at the individual level. This means that if a racially prejudiced person of color in a position of power (e.g., a politician, judge, or police officer) acts in a racially discriminatory or hateful manner, that person cannot be labeled "racist."

On this absurd edifice, CRT scholars additionally assert that all whites are racist,[17] that disagreement or discomfort with this claim is also racist ("white fragility"[18] and "white women's tears"[19]), and that indifference or disinterest in so-called "antiracism" efforts is . . . wait for it . . . racist ("white ignorance,"[20] and "white complicity"[21]). CRT scholars go so far as to assert that it is impossible for white people to engage with people of color in good faith and that common ground can only be found under conditions of converging racial interests.[22]

As noted, these themes are now sufficiently mainstream that questioning them publicly is risky.[23] Recall that Kendi states " . . . I know that for many *racist Americans*, when they see racial disparities, they see black inferiority" (italics added). If this sounds like a threat, you aren't wrong! At the same time, courage is the mother of all virtues, and there are very good reasons why a true opponent of racism would stand up to CRT.

THE CURRENT POLITICAL LANDSCAPE

What happens in California rarely stays in California. As such, we should all be concerned by California's disturbing new "ethnic studies" curriculum[24] under which children will be taught to view America as a "parasitic," "white settler colonist regime." The curriculum's stated purpose is to create "activist intellectuals" who will go on to "decolonize," "deconstruct," and "dismantle" supposedly racist American institutions. As curriculum advocates explain, this program begins in the first grade because children are never too young for indoctrination; indeed, their "inherent empathy" makes them especially vulnerable to it.

Such efforts are not limited to the "granola state"; rather, as documented by researchers such as Christopher Rufo[25] and others,[26] far-Left indoctrination in American schools is legion. CRT activists are clear about their goals. Clarity and focus have given them enormous advantages over most Americans, who are only beginning to notice what has been taking place around them.

Indictments of America, rooted in historic grievances like slavery and Jim Crow, took on greater salience beginning in 2019. This is the year when the *New York Times* magazine empowered Nikole Hannah-Jones to publish a series of essays called the *1619 Project*. Hannah-Jones sought to reframe American history around racial oppression and to cast doubt on America's founding principles and values. To this end, she figuratively changed the date of America's founding from 1776 (the signing of the Declaration of Independence)—or 1789 (the ratification of the Constitution)—to 1619, the year in which the first African slaves were allegedly brought to American shores. Hannah-Jones even argued, much to the chagrin of historians and political scientists, that the Revolutionary War was fought to preserve slavery. Within months, the discredited project had found its way into more than forty-five hundred American classrooms,[27] where it is now helping to instruct the next generation of Americans to hate their country.

Together with publications like the *New York Times*, CRT scholars and advocates have worked to shape an environment where American society is now routinely condemned as "systemically racist" and "white supremacist" by members of the press, the entertainment industry, the political class, and major corporations. Open expressions of hostility toward white Americans— e.g., condemnations of "white privilege" and attacks on "whiteness"—are commonplace as well. Astute media observers will likewise have noticed that violence committed by CRT-friendly (far-Left) groups like BLM and Antifa is often excused, unlike violence committed by right-wing groups (e.g., the Capitol Hill Riot).[28] CRT themes now pervade not only the education establishment,[29] but also workplace diversity training,[30] media and corporate advertising,[31] and entertainment[32] (including children's programming[33] such as *Sesame Street*[34] and Nickelodeon[35]).

In this environment, America recently experienced the worst riots in half a century. Cities were burned. Businesses were looted and destroyed. At least a dozen people were killed[36] and more than $1 billion in property damage was sustained.[37] Core CRT claims regarding alleged oppression in American society provided much of the impetus for this carnage and for its support by so much of the press,[38] media,[39] major corporations,[40] celebrities,[41] and politicians.[42]

CRT is even impacting US foreign policy. Adversaries such as China[43] and Iran[44] leverage CRT claims to diminish American prestige (soft power) and to deflect criticism from their governments' humanitarian abuses. As recently discovered by the Biden Administration during a humiliating exchange[45] with its Chinese counterparts, it is difficult to stand up to such attacks when your opponents repeat your own administration's anti-American rhetoric back to you.[46] The simple truth is that America is being destroyed from within and very few of us presently understand what is happening or know how to fight back in an effective manner. We hope to remedy the situation by doing our small part and by encouraging you to do yours. As a nation, we are stronger together: our national motto is *E Pluribus Unum*, "Out of Many, One."

CRT IN PRACTICE

Consider a recent publication by the Smithsonian National Museum of African American History and Culture titled "Aspects and Assumptions of Whiteness and White Culture."[47] In traditional Marxist thinking, capitalist society sustains itself, in part, by imparting a "false consciousness" on workers to legitimize the social hierarchy and to reduce the likelihood of revolutionary action. In CRT, where race supplants class, false consciousness takes the form of "white culture" and "internalized whiteness." Drawing on such arguments, the Smithsonian lists the following allegedly harmful aspects of whiteness that everyone (including people of color) wrongly internalize and should reject:

- individualism, individual autonomy, and self-reliance
- two-parent homes
- "objective, rational linear thinking"
- causality (i.e., cause -> effect)
- math
- belief that hard work pays off
- property rights
- planning for the future and delaying gratification
- being polite

The Smithsonian is not alone here. In Washington State, the Seattle Public Schools Ethnic Studies Advisory Committee asserts that Western mathematics "disenfranchise people and communities of color."[48] Similar sentiments are echoed by academics[49] and even funded by education reformers such as Bill Gates.[50] In Maryland, training for Montgomery County teachers includes identifying the "damaging characteristics of 'white supremacy culture' including, individualism, objectivity, 'only one right way,' and 'worship of the written word.'"[51] In San Francisco, the vice president of the board of education has condemned as "racist" merit-based selection into advanced academic classes.[52]

According to CRT, science, reason, and objectivity are "white ways of knowing" whereas "black ways of knowing" involve "storytelling" based on "lived experiences."[53] Core elements of white ways of knowing are likewise included in the so-called "master's tools"[54]—institutions that sustain white supremacy, along with things such as the rule of law, due process, civility, keeping to a schedule, etc.

If one sought to sabotage the life prospects of a young person of color (the most vulnerable target of CRT ideas), teaching him or her to reject reason, responsibility, diligence, civility, and the like would do the trick. Credible research demonstrates that the surest path to success in American society is for young people to do precisely the opposite; this is particularly true for people of more moderate means.[55]

CRT's claims are not merely absurd and dangerous, they are racist. By treating rationality, self-restraint, hard work, and responsible time management as the inherent property of whites and not of people of color, CRT attributes adultlike characteristics to whites and childlike characteristics to everyone else. Such arguments should make your average white supremacist blush; indeed, historically speaking, infantilizing people of color in this way provided a useful, paternalistic justification for white supremacy (see: "The White Man's Burden"[56]).

CRT demeans people of color by denying them ownership of and control over their own lives. Worse still, by characterizing ordinary, day-to-day interactions[57] as manifestations of racial oppression, CRT traumatizes many of its adherents. It appears to even function as a kind of reverse cognitive behavioral therapy[58] that makes people more fragile, thereby infantilizing them in reality as well as in theory.[59]

Hopefully, we have piqued your interests by now. It is important for you to understand more about the concept of Critical Race Theory and where it came from so that you can be armed with the knowledge needed to stand up and confront its proponents.

STUDY QUESTIONS

1. How would you explain your opposition to CRT to your local school board?

2. What is educational equity?

3. What would you expect to find in a school curriculum developed to advance cultural competency and learning?

4. Can you think of arguments that might be persuasive in organizing stakeholders interested in defending advanced placement courses and the continued use of entrance exams?

CHAPTER 3

Where Does Critical Race Theory Come From?

CULTURAL MARXISM

MAKE NO MISTAKE ABOUT IT, CRITICAL RACE THEORY POSES AN EXISTENTIAL threat to the United States. It strikes at the very foundations of American society, undermining American unity and common purpose. As noted in the previous chapter, CRT's corrosive qualities are a "feature" rather than a "bug." CRT is a fundamentally, if not orthodoxically, Marxist ideology. It departs from traditional (or "economic") Marxism by substituting social (especially racial) groups for economic groups; however, it retains the larger, Marx-inspired understanding of society as characterized by group power and oppression. It also retains the revolutionary orientation toward politics that logically follows from viewing society in this light.

The origin of this "cultural" Marxist approach can be traced to the writings of the Italian communist, Antonio Gramsci.[1] Gramsci bemoaned Communism's slow advance in the West—a sentiment that would be shared by many Communists to come. Whereas Marx had emphasized the role of material conditions in creating a revolutionary consciousness among workers, Gramsci argued that this process was impeded by the dominance of certain ideas over others ("cultural hegemony").[2]

From this revised footing, Gramsci proposed that capitalism could be overthrown gradually, by infiltrating and transforming society's major institutions—e.g., education establishments, media, law, religion, and the family.[3]

Under new management, the institutions would transmit revolutionary ideas in place of bourgeois ones. As these ideas came to define "common sense" in the public imagination, the old social (and therefore economic) order would decay and give way to a new, revolutionary Communist society (see also: Yuri Bezmenov[4]).

The dark brilliance of weaponizing society's institutions against society itself is that defending society from this attack becomes an act of social deviance. To critique the dominant (counter)culture's assault on gender[5], sexuality[6], marriage[7], and the family[8] is "bigotry," variously defined. To support Christianity, traditional family and sexual norms, and the rule of law is to support institutions of cultural "oppression" and "domination." Indeed, in a culture so profoundly committed to self-immolation, support for the nation itself—e.g., statues of presidents[9] and the American flag[10]—is labeled "divisive" and "racist."

CRITICAL THEORY

Gramsci's banner was carried to America by the Frankfurt School, a group of Marxist and Freudian academics who fled Hitler's Germany in the 1930s. Much as Gramsci had recommended, Frankfurt scholars worked to undermine capitalist society's foundations by attacking ("problematizing") its sociocultural foundations. Their approach has been alternatively described as "neo-Marxist" and as "cultural Marxist," although some consider the latter term to be controversial.[11]

Frankfurt scholars christened their approach "Critical Theory" as a nod to Marx's call for "ruthless criticism of all that exists.[12] The term "critical theory" has both broad and narrow meanings depending on whether the discussion is about philosophy or the history of the social sciences. Max Horkheimer (1937) differentiates a "critical theory"[13] from a "traditional theory" stating that, where the latter attempts to describe the world as it is and to understand how it works, the former begins with a normative moral vision for society, describes how the item being critiqued fails that vision (usually in a systemic sense), and prescribes activism to subvert, dismantle, disrupt, overthrow, or change it—that is, generally, to break and then remake society in accordance with the particular critical theory's prescribed vision.[14]

Using this approach, Frankfurt scholars targeted marriage, the family, and Christianity. In *Eros and Civilization* (1955), for example, Herbert

Marcuse advocates abandoning traditional morality and embracing sexual revolution and gay rights movements.[15] Marcuse was also instrumental in identifying women and racial and sexual minorities as alternative sources of support for revolutionary change.[16] Recentering the oppressor/oppressed paradigm on so-called "victim groups" resolved a problem that had long bedeviled the far Left: the fact that, in the most advanced capitalist country, workers showed little enthusiasm for revolution. Modern identity politics thus owes much to Marcuse's work.[17] Likewise, his arguments for restricting conservative speech in *A Critique of Pure Tolerance* (1969) laid the foundation for political correctness and for the censorship that increasingly pervades American public life.[18]

POSTMODERNISM

Postmodernism is a theory that radically revises "modern assumptions about culture, identity, history, or language."[19] Alongside the Frankfurt School, postmodernism would make key contributions to CRT. Postmodernism emerged during the late 1960s in an environment of destabilizing technological and social change. Postmodern scholars responded to the various crises of modernity—e.g., modern war, decolonization, civil rights struggles, and changing gender and sex norms—by rejecting modernity itself.

As described by Jean-Francois Lyotard in *The Postmodern Condition* (1979), postmodernism fundamentally rejects "metanarratives," or "wide-ranging and cohesive explanations for large phenomena."[20] Science, reason, individualism, and objective standards of value—indeed, objective reality itself—are dismissed by postmodernists as components of an oppressive bourgeois and male-dominated western ideology.

By embracing relativism and rejecting objective reality—and with it, the possibility of obtaining true knowledge—postmodernism insulates itself from criticism and obscures its logical inconsistencies. The theory's most glaring inconsistency is its simultaneous rejection of metanarratives on the one hand and its embrace of a Marxist metanarrative concerning power, oppression, and the imperative of revolutionary change on the other.[21] At the same time, postmodernist scholars reject orthodox Marxism ("scientific socialism") as yet another child of modernity; indeed, Communism's abject and bloody failures were among the crises of modernity that postmodernism emerged to address.[22]

In their struggle against the modern, rational world, postmodernists explore the role played by language as an instrument of social power. Like Frankfurt scholars, they approach their task as activists, seeking out and inverting "power narratives." Michel Foucault, for instance, claims that all knowledge is produced through discourse, or speech promoting a particular worldview.[23] Discourse, in turn, embodies the power interests of society's dominant groups. So understood, it is impossible for knowledge ("power-knowledge") to be value neutral.

Jacques Derrida asserts that language has no objective meaning and that any interpretation of text or speech is equally valid.[24] He further argues that meaning is inherently constructed in terms of opposing positive and negative qualities—e.g., "white" and "male" are good, while "black" and "female" are bad. Consequently, to Derrida, when engaging in an exchange of ideas:

> We are not dealing with the peaceful coexistence of a vis-a-vis, but rather with a violent hierarchy. One of the two terms governs the other (axiologically, logically, etc.), or has the upper hand. To deconstruct the opposition, first of all, is to overturn the hierarchy at a given moment.[25]

Postmodernism's influence on CRT manifests in claims that "speech is violence"[26] (including microaggressions and cancel culture) and in claims that science, reason, and objectivity are "white ways of knowing."[27] It is evident as well in demands to "decolonize"[28] various fields of studies and in the creation of absurdities such as "ethnomathematics."[29]

In *Cynical Theories* (2020), Helen Pluckrose and James Lindsay argue that before postmodernism could successfully impact the larger culture, it first had to resolve its tendency to "deconstruct itself into oblivion."[30] After all, if nothing is real and true knowledge is impossible to obtain, why bother with any of it? The solution offered by Kimberlé Crenshaw was that, if nothing else, structures of racial and gender oppression (and their intersection) were real.[31] Postmodern deconstruction techniques were weaponized on this conceptual footing, first by Critical Legal Studies/Theory and then by Critical Race Theory.[32] These same techniques would also shape gender, queer, and the various ethnic (including "whiteness") "studies" fields.

CRITICAL LEGAL AND RACE THEORIES

CRT's most immediate predecessor is Critical Legal Studies/Theory (CLS), a movement that emerged in the late 1970s in response to a perception among activists that progress toward racial equality had stalled. CLS claims that law creates . . .

> . . . illegitimate social hierarchies, producing domination of women by men, nonwhites by whites, and the poor by the wealthy. They claim that apparently neutral language and institutions, operated through law, mask relationships of power and control. The emphasis on individualism within the law similarly hides patterns of power relationships while making it more difficult to summon up a sense of community and human interconnection.[33]

CLS uses the law to attack society ("hierarchical structures"[34]), going after such things as procedural equality, market freedom, property rights, and, indeed, rights *per se*, consistent with its opposition to individualism.[35] CLS is, in effect, Critical Theory as applied to law, drawing heavily on postmodernist interpretation and deconstruction techniques to dismantle the law itself. As the child of CLS, CRT inherits this same approach while also drawing on radical feminism (e.g., social constructivism[36]) and Whiteness Studies (e.g., Privilege Theory[37] and White Fragility[38]).

Arriving finally at CRT, we encounter the most expressly political and least intellectual branch of the cultural Marxist family tree. CRT's crude pragmatism sometimes obscures its philosophical roots. Consider for example, the use of "storytelling" to create counter-narratives to facts and evidence, or consider demands for censorship of political speech (see, Richard Delgado for both).[39] Neither position is particularly "highbrow"; yet, recall that postmodernists reasoned their way to rejecting reason (along with science and evidence) as components of white, male, bourgeois oppression. Likewise, regarding censorship, recall Derrida's claim that all speech creates power-based binaries, privileging some categories (e.g., people) over others.

Along similar lines, when one encounters from CRT seemingly absurd and irrational claims—e.g., that colorblindness and meritocracy are racist or that desegregation did little to help American blacks[40]—or transparently harmful advice such as encouraging minorities to reject hard work and time-liness ("internalized whiteness"),[41] recall that the purpose of a critical theory, per Horkheimer, is to break society and then to remake it along different lines. CRT advocates are acting in accordance with that purpose. Their ideas don't have to make sense to be dangerous.

Lastly, given that this chapter traces CRT's intellectual traditions, we feel that it bears emphasizing that all of theseambient raina traditions are antithetical and diametrically opposed to the ideas and values that form the American tradition.[42] We explore this conflict in greater detail in the next two chapters.

STUDY QUESTIONS

1. What is cultural Marxism and how did it become a factor in American society?

2. How does cultural Marxism differ from economic Marxism?

3. Name the major theorists who helped develop cultural Marxism.

4. What connection does Critical Legal Studies have to Critical Race Theory?

CHAPTER 4

Critical Race Theory and Traditional American Values

UN-AMERICAN VALUES

CRT SHOCKS THE SENSIBILITIES OF MANY AMERICANS, ESPECIALLY THOSE WHO hold to traditional American values and principles. CRT proponents bully[1], shame[2], and intimidate K-12 school children no less than adults forced into "diversity"/"cultural sensitivity" training. Such practices continue despite research confirming the harmful effects of shaming and bullying children in classrooms and in other contexts. If this harassment was targeted toward members of designated racial or ethnic minority groups, it would be roundly condemned. Racial double standards should never be accepted; yet, it often seems that double standards are the *only* standards, for example, in cases of violence and other aggression against whites and, often, Asians.[3]

Consider the dozen or so lawsuits recently filed against CRT-enforcing schools and businesses.[4] In one case, white employees were instructed to "step back and yield to colleagues of color" as well as to view their own culture as "inherently supremacist." In Illinois, seventh- and eighth-grade students were told to remain silent and to lower their eyes—a gesture of submission—while being addressed by their CRT instructor. In New York City, white employees were told by instructors that their racial identity is "toxicity in the air." In Nevada, a twelfth grader was required to announce and degrade aspects of his identity, including his Christian faith.

There is a name we commonly use to describe bullying and shaming people in this manner: we call such behavior "un-American." To describe something as un-American is to say that it is antithetical to some important aspect of American traditions and values. Labeling something un-American can be controversial—see, The House Un-American Activities Committee[5] —but, as a logical matter, if American nationhood and identity derive principally from certain ideas and practices, antithetical ideas and practices are un-American, by definition.

Take, for example, President Biden's use of the label "un-American" to condemn anti-Semitic harassment[6] and to condemn assaults on Asian Americans.[7] In this regard, the president is absolutely correct. Any such mistreatment of our fellow citizens on account of immutable characteristics (e.g., race) or beliefs (including religion) is a violation of our common understanding of who we are as a people. Harassment, discrimination, intimidation, and general intolerance directed toward whites, Christians, men, and other groups deemed "oppressors" by their attackers likewise fit this bill. It doesn't matter what the perpetrators of such abuse call themselves or how they rationalize their abuse—their behavior is indefensible.

Accordingly, in his executive memorandum banning CRT training in executive departments and agencies, President Trump condemned CRT as "un-American" and as "anti-American," an even harsher charge.[8] Given the examples referenced here, the former president is on firm ground where CRT *in practice* is concerned, but what about CRT *in theory*? Are CRT's proponents in our nation's schools and workplaces simply applying their doctrine in a ham-fisted way or is there something fundamentally un/anti-American about the doctrine itself from which the abusive nature of its practical application derives?

We address this question here and in the next chapter by exploring the values and principles that establish the American tradition and by evaluating the compatibility of CRT with that tradition. We begin with America's secular traditions and then consider America's religious traditions in chapter 5.

CLASSICAL LIBERALISM

Classical liberalism is a philosophy that promotes protecting civil liberties and limiting the role of government.[9] It is fundamental to American democracy; CRT, however, strongly rejects this tradition. In this way, Critical Race

Theory is anti-American in the same way that the sky is blue and water is wet. To their credit, CRT advocates do little to hide this. In their introduction, Delgado and Stefancic write, "unlike traditional civil rights discourse, which stresses incrementalism and step-by-step progress, Critical Race Theory questions the very foundations of the liberal order, including equality theory, legal reasoning, Enlightenment rationalism, and neutral principles of constitutional law."[10] They state further that CRT proponents "are suspicious of another liberal mainstay, namely, rights" and that "classical liberalism is overly caught up in the search for universals."

By the "liberal order," "classical liberalism," and of course, "rights," Delgado and Stefancic refer to the principles underlying the American system: those enshrined in the Declaration of Independence. These include equality under law ("equality theory") and individual rights naturally belonging to all people ("universals"), as informed by a rational (Enlightenment) understanding of the world and by republican traditions of self-government. Rejecting this tradition, opposition to freedom (e.g., speech[11] and property rights[12]), individualism[13], meritocracy[14], the rule of law[15], impartial justice[16], and even equality[17] are consistent themes in CRT scholarship and advocacy. Proposals for mass property confiscation and race-based redistribution[18] and for a federal Department of Antiracism[19] superseding all laws and government action (i.e., democracy) illustrate the tyrannical and even totalitarian tendencies that befit a movement descended from Marxism.

At this point, we return to our previous observations regarding abusive practices inflicted in the name of "antiracism." The standard for understanding such practices as "un-American" is clearly established by the principles encoded in America's founding documents and by the classical liberal tradition that animates them. CRT conflicts with that standard in theory, as well as in application in workforce training and in K-12 instruction. Stated differently, CRT is a fundamentally anti-American doctrine that informs and animates un-American behavior.

ALLEGATIONS OF WHITE SUPREMACY

We once knew what a white supremacist was. It was a white person who believed that membership in the Caucasian race made him or her genetically and morally superior to members of other racial and ethnic groups. This was the understanding in 2002, when my book *The New White Nationalism in America* was published.[20] In that book, I (Carol) warned about identity politics and multiculturalism movements that encouraged racial identification among Americans of color. At the time, I was not familiar enough with CRT to make connections that seem obvious now. It was clear, however, that no good thing would come from identity politics. What I called for was an embrace of the American national identity where we would put the interests of the whole nation above our perceived group interests.

Fast forward to today: CRT has redefined the concept of white supremacy and given it an entirely new meaning encompassing nearly all white people. Now being born into the white race automatically makes one a supremacist unless one is explicitly *anti-white*. Indeed, CRT is a total rejection of America's liberal tradition in terms of how we ought to treat each other as morally equal and autonomous individuals in possession of natural rights.

On this basis, CRT levels false allegations against our nation and so we think it is important for us to directly address the claim that the United States—and therefore, American identity—is somehow rooted in white supremacy. This claim is plainly anti-American and false. To begin, when thinking of national identity, it is helpful to separately consider its "ethnic" and "civic" components. The ethnic sources of national identity refer to a shared heritage and include such things as a common language, faith, and ancestry. Civic sources refer to common institutions and values.[21]

America's diversity and relative youth (245 years) limit the ethnic contribution to national identity. Americans do share a common culture, language, customs, and traditions, including those derived from a widely shared Judeo-Christian religious inheritance. In this regard, the influence of America's "Old Stock" (Anglo-Saxons) looms large; but contributions from other groups, including people of color, are also unmistakable. To take just one example, consider the outsized role played by black Americans in shaping the nation's music (e.g., blues, jazz, rock and roll, and hip hop), culture, sports, and vernacular.

Without question, American national identity is primarily understood along civic lines. As described by Abraham Lincoln, the United States was "conceived in liberty and dedicated to the proposition that all men are created equal."[22] America's creedal identity creates a foundation for "Americanness" in the principles of liberty, individualism, equality, and popular government, rather than in a shared ethnic or racial heritage.[23] These are universal principles "applicable to all men and all times."[24]

Such an understanding of what it means to be American is plainly at odds with racial supremacism. A white supremacist opposes natural equality in principle and opposes liberty, popular government, and individualism in practice by denying fundamental rights and liberties to his or her fellow citizens. Racial oppression under slavery and Jim Crow contradicted the nation's founding principles and so stained its identity. Racial oppression today is likewise un-American. Far from a fig leaf for white supremacy, American values are the reason why *true* systemic racism—slavery and Jim Crow—was ultimately unsustainable in the United States.

Frederick Douglass understood this fact;[25] indeed, he weaponized[26] the contradiction between American values and chattel slavery by calling whites to task for failing to live up to their nation's founding and purpose.[27] Martin Luther King Jr. did the same while also emphasizing the contradiction between racial oppression and America's Judeo-Christian inheritance.[28] The great moral crusades for abolition and civil rights were waged on behalf of American principles.[29]

CRT-inspired efforts such as the *New York Times's 1619 Project*[30] distort American history by treating aberrations from founding principles as founding principles themselves. Such efforts are, moreover, riddled with factual errors,[31] including:

- the preposterous claim that the American Revolution was fought to preserve slavery (disregarding the *New York Times's* own fact-checker[32]),

- egregious misrepresentations of Abraham Lincoln's views on equality, and

- crediting slavery for American prosperity when slavery almost certain stalled economic development in the South.[33]

The *1619 Project* absurdly attributes nearly every real and supposed evil in American society to the institution of slavery, from capitalist excesses to the absence of single-payer healthcare and even traffic jams. Moreover, even the *date itself* is wrong. The first Africans brought to America in 1619 were not slaves but rather indentured servants. After fulfilling their contracts, some of these previously indentured servants—all blacks themselves—contracted black and white indentured servants of their own.[34]

This isn't to diminish the history of racial oppression in the United States. Acknowledging that history is important, but it is likewise important to understand the larger context. Consider, for example, that:

- Slavery predated America's founding by *literally all of human history.*

- Slavery was largely stamped out by the United States and Great Britain.

- In so doing, the US and Britain acted at great cost and in accordance with their own universalistic, individualistic values—the same values loathed by CRT.

- In times (e.g., antiquity) and places (e.g., the Middle East) lacking such values, slavery was nearly ubiquitous.[35]

The tragedy of CRT's spread throughout the American body politic is that Americans are now losing sight of their country's true history and of the remarkable racial progress it has made. A recent study by Eric Kaufmann finds that exposure to news and social media (where CRT themes are legion[36]) promotes exaggerated perceptions of racism.[37] Kaufmann additionally finds that CRT discourse demoralizes blacks by reducing self-perceptions of agency. Other research[38] shows that exposing right-leaning whites to CRT themes increases ethnocentrism and ingroup identification: the predicates for white nationalism (e.g., the Alt Right).[39] Just as America's triumphs are testament to one set of ideas, its present difficulties are testament to another.

In the United States of America, citizens enjoy equality under law, protections of individual rights, and opportunities for success that continue to inspire envy from people around the world. In this context, we think that CRT-led efforts to label the United States a "white supremacist" country should be viewed as a kind of modern "blood libel." We do not say this lightly: the blood libel reference historically refers to grotesque accusations leveled against Jewish people by anti-Semites.[40] Such accusations were unfounded, obscene, and used as a predicate for attacks against an entire group of people. Contemporary attacks on American identity are (and do) the same.

We have made references to Christianity in light of CRT's attacks on Christians. In the next chapter, we examine America's Christian heritage and why Christians often find themselves in the crosshairs of CRT's proponents.

STUDY QUESTIONS

1. What un-American tactics do CRT proponents use to spread their message?

2. What is classical liberalism, and how does CRT reject it?

3. What is the American identity according to CRT advocates?

4. Is CRT opposed to American values in theory, in practice, or in both theory and practice?

CHAPTER 5

Critical Race Theory and America's Christian Inheritance

CHRISTIANITY IN THE "AMERICAN CREED"

POLITICS IS FAMOUSLY DOWNSTREAM FROM CULTURE.[1] A LESSER-KNOWN BUT important dictum is that culture is downstream from the "cult"—or from *religion*, in the original Latin. Any serious discussion of American values and traditions must therefore address the role of Christianity in the American Creed. In doing so, our intention is *emphatically not* to suggest that non-Christian Americans are, in any sense, less authentically American; we aim rather to more fully account for the context in which American values and principles developed. Much like America's (ostensibly secular) liberal political inheritance, we find Christianity to be plainly incompatible with Critical Race Theory; however, understanding why this is the case requires some unpacking.

Christianity has shaped the United States in at least four important respects. The first and most obvious is the direct influence of Christianity—and of its antecedent, Judaism—on American culture through the faith traditions of the American people. Settlers of the American colonies were almost exclusively Christian, and influential settler groups (e.g., the Puritans and Quakers) were devoutly so. Consequently, Christianity helped shape the nation's laws, holidays, and customs. Prominent institutions (e.g., universities[2]) were founded with the aim of teaching faith and promoting Christian understandings of public virtue. Christian imagery is prominently

37

displayed on public buildings. Government proceedings begin with public prayers, and so forth.

Christianity's direct role in American public life is also expressed in the nation's "covenantal tradition."[3] Covenants are enduring agreements between parties meant to be stronger than contracts—e.g., God's covenant with the Israelites.[4] Consistent with their descriptions of America as a "new Israel," many of America's founders held covenantal views of the United States.

Such views, in turn, inform the second distinct source of Christian influence in America: the "civil religion." As described by Robert Bellah, the civil religion is the United States' institutionalized, national public faith, which is distinct from the "private" religions of the American people.[5] The civil religion is a kind of "Christianity-lite" that draws from the nation's Judeo-Christian faith traditions and from Christianity's influence on the American founding[6] (more on this to follow) to frame the nation's purpose in biblical terms. Examples include:

- presidential addresses evoking God;
- public policy advocacy (e.g., voting rights reform[7]) framed in terms of carrying out "God's will";
- the consecration of American history with biblical analogies: e.g., independence as "exodus" and Lincoln's death (martyrdom) for the nation's sin of slavery as akin to Jesus's death for the sins of mankind.

Third, America's decentralized and limited system of government reflects the framers' view[8] (perhaps excluding Jefferson[9]) that religion would supplement state power in preserving social order. As stated by Washington in his *Farewell Address*:

> Of all the dispositions and habits which lead to political prosperity, Religion and Morality are indispensable supports. . . . A volume could not trace all their connections with private and public felicity. . . . And let us with caution indulge the supposition that morality can be maintained without religion. Whatever may be conceded to the influence of refined education on minds of peculiar structure, reason, and experience both forbid us to expect that National morality can prevail in exclusion of religious principle.[10]

Putting the matter more succinctly, John Adams says, "Our Constitution is made only for a moral and religious people. It is wholly inadequate to the government of any other."[11] Self-government, in other words, presupposes a self-governing citizenry. Averting anarchy requires some restraint over individuals' more pathological inclinations: excessive ambition, greed, cruelty, lust, retribution, etc. Limited government means that control must also exist apart from the state: in strong communities, in families, and within citizens themselves.

Given that, at the time, nearly every American was a Christian,[12] it is safe to assume that Washington and Adams meant "Christianity" when referring to "religion." Many today would balk at this understanding; however, as recorded by Alexis de Tocqueville in *Democracy in America* (1835), American society flourished under this arrangement.[13] Some, perhaps channeling President Eisenhower, might amend the framers' view to say that *any* religious belief can carry the weight of private and public morality in a free society.[14]

Fourth, Christianity not only provides (or provid*ed*) the guardrails around the liberal political tradition, it also shaped the development of that tradition. Consider that, as noted by Bellah (1967), the Declaration of Independence—the heart of the nation's purpose and "creed"—references God in four distinct ways:

- as the designer of the universe and source of natural law
- as the source of humanity's inalienable rights contra absolutism
- as the Supreme Judge of the world
- as the source of divine providence

The Declaration was hardly the exception to some general, secular rule. Christianity exerted a profound influence on political thought in late eighteenth-century America; indeed, a survey of more than fifteen thousand political pamphlets, articles, and books of that era finds that America's founding fathers referred to the Bible more often than they referred to all Enlightenment thinkers combined.[15] Americans had also been practicing democracy (in varying degrees) for centuries by this point, and Protestantism's influence on democratic participation appears to have been substantial.[16]

The West's secular liberal inheritance also owes much to its Christian religious inheritance. As a movement away from superstition and toward science and materialism, the Enlightenment is typically framed in opposition to Christianity.[17] There are problems with this account, however, including the fact that the intellectual and private commitments of many Enlightenment thinkers were often deeply Christian.[18]

More fundamentally, it is difficult to imagine how one arrives at liberalism or, for that matter, a notion of a rationally ordered and discernable universe, without a firm grounding in natural law. Natural law is deeply woven into the Christian faith—it is dogma in Catholicism, for example. Describing natural law in *Summa Theologiae* (1485), Saint Thomas Aquinas writes, "The light of reason is praise by nature [and thus by God] in every man to guide him in his acts."[19] Through reason, people discern the truth about God's creation.

The Christian tradition places natural law above "positive" or man-made law, enabling earthly rulers to be held to account. Natural law laid the groundwork for rejecting absolutism,[20] for asserting claims of immutable rights,[21] and for proposing contractual theories of government. So, while Thomas Jefferson drew heavily on John Locke's *Second Treatise* (1689) in the Declaration's preface, both men's writings testify to Christianity's influence on the classical liberal mind.[22]

Political theorists Ofir Haivry and Yoram Hazony go further, arguing that much of what we commonly credit to the Enlightenment and to liberalism should be credited instead to a distinct, but also biblically rooted, pre-liberal English conservative tradition.[23] In *The Virtue of Nationalism* (2018), Hazony additionally credits the "Protestant construction of the West," as manifested in the Peace of Westphalia for institutionalizing protections for individual rights and national self-determination.[24]

Taken together, the influence of Christian thinking on classically liberal and conservative values is profound. Given the institutionalization of these values in the United States, CRT's hostility to the American Creed is likewise aimed at America's Christian religious inheritance.

THE CHURCH(ES) OF WOKE

This is not to say that Critical Race Theory is only *indirectly* opposed to Christianity. Consider, for example, the distinction drawn by Ibram X. Kendi between, in his words, "liberation" and "savior" theologies.[25] Kendi describes the former as a commitment to radical social activism, as informed by a vision of Jesus Christ as a political revolutionary struggling against oppression. He describes the latter as one where individual sinners are saved through their faith in Jesus Christ. Christian and non-Christian readers alike will recognize Christianity in "savior theology."

Kendi goes on to assert that "antiracists" (CRT advocates) must reject savior theology (Christianity, traditionally understood) because it . . .

> . . . goes right in line with racist ideals and racist theology in which they say, you know what, black people . . . other racial groups, the reason why they're struggling on earth is because what they are behaviorally doing wrong and it is my job as the pastor to sort of save these wayward black people or wayward poor people or wayward queer people. That type of theology breeds bigotry.[26]

Kendi's claims here are consistent with his earlier referenced claims regarding the meaning of racial disparities. "Sin" is to be found in oppressive power structures, not in individual people. It certainly doesn't reside in the *victims* of oppression.

The following attempts to catalogue the conflicts between Christianity and CRT, borrowing heavily from Christian apologetics blogger Neil Shenvi.[27] Given the deep incongruity of these two metanarratives, this list is almost certainly not comprehensive:

1. Hegemonic narratives

First and most obviously, CRT derives from atheist thinkers who viewed Christianity as an instrument of capitalist (and racist, sexist, heteronormative, cisgender, etc.) oppression. Second, a consistent theme in CRT is its distrust of authoritative claims, particularly those perceived as deriving from dominant groups. We thus encounter claims that math is racist[28] and science is a white "way of knowing."[29] As Shenvi amusingly puts it, "Unfortunately, the Bible is nothing but one giant, colossal hegemonic discourse from start to finish. . . . That means there is one true story of religion, one true story of morality, one true story of sexuality, one true story of gender, and so forth."[30] It can be added that the truth or falsehood of biblical narratives is not contingent on one's "lived experiences."

2. The problem of sin versus the problem of oppression

In the biblical view, free will creates the possibility (inevitability) of disobedience to God's will. The problem of sin resides in the heart of every person, individually. The obligation to stop sinning and to seek redemption through faith is, likewise, an individual one. In the CRT view, society is comprised of groups arrayed in unequal power relationships. The problem of the world is oppression; specifically, oppression of *groups by groups*. As such, individual agency is radically deemphasized.

3. Fundamental enmity or Christian equality

As noted, CRT is surprisingly opposed to equality.[31] This follows from its division of society into mutually antagonistic groups. In the Christian worldview, by contrast, "there is neither Jew nor Gentile, neither slave nor free, nor is there male and female, for you are all one in Christ Jesus" (Galatians 3:28). People are not natural enemies but rather brothers and sisters in Christ, each being made in God's image, and each being guilty of sin and in need of salvation. Of course, theory is one thing and practice is another. "Your experience may differ," as the saying goes; but, beginning in different places, it shouldn't be surprising when Christians and Marxists arrive at different destinations.[32]

4. Moral universalism versus moral asymmetry

A corollary to the previous point is that, as a group-power metanarrative[33] that rejects objective ("hegemonic") standards of value, CRT jettisons individual/universal ethics for relativism. This puts CRT at odds with both Christianity and liberalism (natural law).

CRT relies on extraordinary and conspiratorial rationalizations of unequal treatment in theory, but there's no denying its demand for unequal treatment in practice.[34] For example, speech[35] and behavior[36] are either excused/praised or condemned depending on the group-interests they allegedly advance. This asymmetry extends to this moral realm where members of oppressor and oppressed groups are assigned different obligations and are judged according to different criteria. Some people are obliged to publicly grovel for sins they never committed (e.g., slavery) and renounce their supposed privileges.[37] Other people are condescendingly excused from responsibility for even *their own* actions, let alone those of other group members.[38]

5. Separate kingdoms

Even Christianity's most committed critics readily acknowledge[39] the importance of Jesus's injunction to "Render unto Caesar the things that are Caesar's, and unto God the things that are God's" (Mathew 22:21). Like the Constitution's separate powers, separate kingdoms are essential to liberty. The separation of political and religious authority—codified in the First Amendment—doesn't banish God (religious expression) from the public sphere any more than it banishes Caesar (politics) from the private sphere; rather, it resists the unity of the two authorities (god-kings), thereby safeguarding a private sphere of life from the possibility of *total* power in the hands of a single authority.

CRT is not concerned with the supernatural, but this is not a *limiting* principle. Rather, as with other radical perspectives,[40] the personal is political. Religious tests for public office are not permitted in America nor are they permitted in the private sector, apart from narrow exceptions for explicitly religious organizations.[41] By contrast, public- and private-sector workers are often forced to attend CRT indoctrination sessions under the guise of "workforce diversity training." Likewise, religious instruction is not permitted in public schools,[42] but CRT is embedded in curricula around the country.[43] All must bend the knee in CRT's singular kingdom; yet, even if CRT were to triumph completely—e.g., if Americans traded self-government for Kendi's antiracist tyranny—would its crusade end there? If America is truly racism and white supremacy "all the way down," where does CRT stop?[44]

Critical Race Theory is, functionally speaking, a new religion. This observation was prominently made in 2015 by John McWhorter, noting that "antiracism" (in his phrasing) contains the core elements of religion, including faith (suspension of disbelief), a creed, a clergy, rituals, proselytizing, judgment, redemption, and even original sin.[45] The last three elements are noteworthy in that they are not merely religious but are specifically Christian in character. This point is powerfully developed by Joshua Mitchell in *American Awakening* (2020). Mitchell attributes the ascendance of "identity politics"[46] to the decline of mainline Protestantism. The new faith borrows from the old (from Protestantism, specifically) notions of transgression and innocence but, unfortunately, not forgiveness, charity, or humility. It thus constructs a "ghastly and unworkable manifestation of Christianity" where sinner-groups are redeemed and where saint-groups are confined to a permanent state of impotent rage.

Returning to Bellah's analysis, it could be argued that CRT is not *a* new religion but is actually *two* new religions: one public replacement for America's "civil religion" and one private "Woke Church" expressed in various denominations, through CRT's colonization and subversion of Christianity proper.

Examples of the former abound in the Biden Administration, where America is condemned as "systemically racist" with the kind of zeal displayed by former administrations in praising America as a "shining city on the hill."[47] Consider, for example, Press Secretary Jen Psaki's remarkable public confession of faith ("suspension of disbelief," in McWhorter's terms) evoking systemic racism to condemn a police officer for acting to save the life of a black teenager by shooting the person who was *trying to stab her with a knife* (the assailant was also black).[48] CRT has given us a new national story of America's founding and purpose, and our institutions are dutifully expounding that story. Monuments to the greatness of American history are thus coming down.

In terms of Christianity itself, the creeping influence of CRT on doctrine is unmistakable. In evangelical Christianity, this "Woke Church" holds that whites carry a special inherited sin as descendants of slave owners and beneficiaries of systemic racism. Whites must therefore seek *earthly* redemption[49] by tearing down systems of oppression and by giving money to black people in reparations.[50] Catholicism is no less affected[51] and, as argued by Joseph Bottum in *An Anxious Age* (2014), mainline Protestantism has led the way.[52]

The church should be leading the fight against CRT. In Acts 17:26, Luke reminds fellow believers that "from one man he made all the nations, that they should inhabit the whole earth; and he marked out their appointed times in history and the boundaries of their lands." In *Countercultural Living*, I (Carol) wrote:

> As a worldview, Critical Theory—along with all of its off-shoots like Critical Race Theory (CRT)—is at odds with the biblical message of Jesus Christ's finished work on the cross. Christians believe that human beings are created in God's divine image and that we are all sinners in need of the redeeming power of Jesus's shed blood on the cross. The Critical Theory worldview speaks of oppressive dominant

groups and marginalized minority groups needing liberation. Such deliverance, according to Critical Theory, can only be granted by the dominant groups, who are expected to divest themselves of their privilege, power, and wealth. In these narratives, ethnic and racial minorities fall into the category of the oppressed. Whites and Western civilization, in particular, fall into the category of oppressors who must continually make amends for societal racism.[53]

CRT preaches a different gospel. It should not be leading and guiding the work of the church. The church needs to lead in this area. We hope that this chapter has helped you understand CRT's anti-biblical narrative and the harm it is wreaking on Christianity and its witness to the world.

STUDY QUESTIONS

1. How has Christianity shaped the United States?

2. What are the conflicts between Christianity and Critical Race Theory?

3. Why is CRT essentially a new religion?

4. Why should the church be a key player in the fight against CRT?

CHAPTER 6

Critical Race Theory, the U.S. Constitution, and Civil Rights Law

CRT VS CIVIL RIGHTS

IN CRITICAL RACE THEORY, WE FIND A MOVEMENT WILLING TO TRAMPLE RIGHTS, liberties, and national solidarity in pursuit of *equity*: equal outcomes and distributions of goods by group. To recap,[1] CRT proponents object to the First Amendment's elevation of free speech above "the freedom to be free from the victimization, stigma, and humiliation that free speech entails."[2] The concern here is not hateful speech *per se*, but specifically speech targeting members of "oppressed groups."[3] CRT likewise opposes equality ("mere nondiscrimination") and individual rights as impediments to remedies for group imbalances—e.g., confiscating property from whites and giving it to blacks.[4] In terms of justice, CRT rejects the idea that laws should apply equally to everyone ("legal neutrality")[5] and instead embraces an individualized "justice" that, again, attempts to remedy group disparities.[6] Finally, CRT puts democracy in the crosshairs; after all, why should we let inequitable policies stand just because the majority chose them?[7]

CRT's opposition to liberties, rights, and to the rule of law is in obvious tension with the civil rights movement, which fought to secure civil rights and equality under law for people of color.[8] Its attack on civil rights deprives people of color of their inheritance no less than whites; however, proponents like Derrick Bell argue that abstractions and legal remedies do little to advance minority interests or well-being. Laws, in this view, simply encode their authors' (dominant groups') interests.[9] Bell's "racial realism" consequently embraces an "ends justify the means" approach to legal reasoning, substituting the rule of law with the rule of men. CRT proponents should consider whether this approach is likely to benefit racial minorities in the long run, in a democracy, where majority rule is restrained by structures such as rights, equality, and legal neutrality.

CRT's radicalism speaks to its despair regarding the legacy of the civil rights movement. As noted in chapter 3, Critical Legal Studies (CLS) was formed in response to perceptions that civil rights gains were eroding. CLS and subsequently, CRT, pinpointed the problem on the American political system, society, and values—a framework within which the civil rights movement was also embedded.[10] As stated by Kimberlé Crenshaw, "Liberals and conservatives seemed to see issues of race and law from within the same structure of analysis—namely, a policy that legal rationality could identify and eradicate the biases of race consciousness in social decision-making."[11] A line of continuity thus links the colorblind ideal at the heart of debates over affirmative action to MLK's "I Have a Dream" speech and, from there, to Justice John Marshall Harlan's dissent to the doctrine of "separate but equal" in *Plessy v. Ferguson* (1896).[12] As argued in chapter 4, that line ultimately traces back to the American founding.

CRT VS THE CONSTITUTION AND CIVIL RIGHTS LAW

The conflict between CRT and civil rights and liberties is presently playing out in the judicial system. Under CRT instruction in schools and workplaces, whites (including young children[13]) are berated by instructors and required to confess culpability for racial oppression.[14] Those who fail to do so, or who protest their innocence, are further condemned for manifesting "white fragility"—additional complicity in racism.[15] Disagreeing with CRT claims of systemic racism and white supremacy likewise exposes students and employees to public scolding[16] and retribution.[17]

Such practices raise important constitutional and legal concerns. Compelling speech rather obviously violates free speech protections under the First Amendment. Punishing employees and students for noncompliance with unconstitutional requirements, in turn, violates Fourteenth Amendment due process protections. Singling out racial (and other) groups for hostile treatment seems to plainly violate the Civil Rights Act of 1964,[18] which prohibits discrimination on the basis of "race, color, religion, sex, or national origin," and under Titles VI[19] and IX[20] of the 1972 Education Amendments to that act, which extend these prohibitions to institutions receiving federal funding (e.g., schools).

In response to these apparent civil rights violations, a network of conservative organizations and attorneys[21] is backing a series of lawsuits[22] that seeks to abolish[23] CRT indoctrination in the federal government and in the nation's schools and workplaces. Among them, a Nevada lawsuit alleges that a high school student was required to announce aspects of his identity and then to denigrate those identity markers using terms such as "privileged" and "oppressor."[24] Refusing to do so, he was given a failing grade. Another lawsuit alleges that New York City's Department of Education "silenced, sidelined, and punished plaintiffs and other Caucasian female DOE employees on the basis of their race, gender, and unwillingness to accept their other colleagues' hateful stereotypes about them."[25] In California, a lawsuit against the Department of Fish and Wildlife claims that employees were compelled to affirm CRT claims regarding whites' "inherent racism."[26]

DISINGENUOUS DEFENSES

At the time of this writing, CRT proponents have responded to anti-CRT lawsuits with the following challenges. First, defenders claim[27] that such efforts violate the First Amendment free speech rights of schools and companies, including those of the contractors who run the various "diversity, equity, and inclusivion" (DEI) workshops.[28] They extend this claim, asserting that CRT's opponents do not believe in the legal merits of their own lawsuits but are rather cynically attempting to mobilize conservative voters by picking a fight in the "culture war."[29] Second, CRT proponents argue that efforts to restrict CRT, including President Trump's now-revoked executive order[30], limit the employment opportunities of DEI contractors and threaten the DEI business model. Third, they argue that restriction bills employ vague wording. Finally, as one might expect, CRT proponents argue that anti-CRT efforts are motivated by racism. A New Hampshire bill (HB 544),[31] which limits workplace CRT instruction, was thus labeled the "White Supremacy Protection Act" by its opponents.[32]

Regarding the claims of CRT defenders, the latter three do not merit extended consideration here. The wording of specific bills is a technical question. Allegations of racism are par for the course when challenging CRT. Finally, regarding the viability of the DEI business model, if a given firm's services are no longer desired, that, as they say, is that.

As a legal matter, the First Amendment objection is at least *potentially* serious, even if CRT proponents are plainly disingenuous. The irony of defending an anti-free speech movement on free speech grounds will be lost on very few. As noted, the CRT case against free speech evokes the emotional distress—"victimization, stigma, and humiliation," in Derrick Bell's words—people may feel when confronted with ideas with which they disagree. This is, without question, one of the costs of freedom. One can certainly sympathize with those who, from an abundance of empathy, weigh the costs and benefits of free speech differently than the framers; however, in the case of CRT proponents, one finds little evidence of empathy for white people—children included—experiencing emotional distress as a result of being forced to endure racially motivated verbal harassment in institutional settings (institutional racism?). Indeed, CRT proponents treat such distress ("white fragility" and "white tears") as a cynical ploy by whites to avoid confronting their complicity in racism.[33]

Regarding the legal merits of the First Amendment argument, lawyer and author Hans Bader demonstrates that CRT is on shaky ground.[34] The most obvious problem is that courts have ruled that government entities such as school boards do not have First Amendment rights.[35] The Supreme Court has also ruled that states may determine school curricula and that doing so does not raise free speech concerns.[36] Indeed, the Court has affirmed that the powers of political subdivisions (e.g., school boards) reside "in the absolute discretion of the State."[37]

Not only *can* states prohibit CRT instruction in schools but there is also a strong argument that they *must* do so. As Bader states, "the Fourteenth Amendment forbids states to create a learning environment that is hostile to students based on their race or sex—such as by repeatedly subjecting a captive audience of students to racist or sexist insults."[38] In this regard, the definition of racism (and sexism) matters. The CRT understanding by which only whites can be racist is plainly *not* the position encoded in civil rights law; rather, whites are afforded equal protection under the law and are therefore protected from racial harassment[39] and discrimination.[40] The First Amendment prohibits compelling speech in school settings,[41] and this presumably protects white students no less than students of color.[42]

CRT in the workplace is also legally problematic, though its proponents might have more leeway as there are potentially important distinctions to consider.[43] Inviting a speaker to a conference where attendance is optional is one thing. Requiring attendance at such a conference or contracting with such a speaker to lead employee training sessions is another, given that absent or passive employees will be noticed by managers.

Case law seems to suggest that common DEI training practices constitute "racial harassment." Take, for example, Sandia National Laboratories' mandatory "3-day reeducation camp for white males."[44] White male employees were instructed to expose the roots of white male culture, publicly recite "white privilege" and "male privilege" statements, and then to write apology letters to "white women, people of color, and other groups."[45]

In the Sandia case, an employee was suspended for criticizing this training. Bader argues that such action likely violates anti-retaliation provisions of civil rights law.[46] This is important because even if DEI instruction of this kind is somehow *not* racial harassment, mandatory training presupposes punishment for noncompliance. Given that case law protects employees from retaliation in cases where they might reasonably believe that their civil rights have been violated, mandating attendance at such events could prove legally impractical.[47]

Much like CRT's legal defense, its ethical defense in the mainstream press outlets appears insincere. These sources routinely describe CRT worksite training and school instruction in euphemistic terms such as "racial sensitivity training"[48] or "racial inequality education."[49] Intentionally or otherwise, such descriptions mask CRT's inherent divisiveness. When describing the ideology itself, prominent news sources appeal to opposition to racism and other nearly universally revered values.[50] An interview in *The Washington Post* even evoked founding principles as a defense of CRT.[51] The profound irony of such accounts is that such values are *nearly* universal (rather than universal) chiefly due to sustained efforts by CRT advocates and other cultural Marxists to delegitimize them.

As argued by Christopher Rufo, if CRT defenders are confident in the force of their ideas, they will defend them, not with platitudes and not only in theory, but specifically and in practice.[52] They will assert, for example:

- that teachers should instruct third-graders to deconstruct their racial and sexual identities, and to rank themselves according to power and privilege;[53]

- that principals should tell parents to become "white traitors" and to support "white abolition"[54]; and

- that companies should instruct white employees to "be less white," and so forth.[55]

A few prominent proponents are willing to speak plainly in support of CRT. To his credit, Ibram X. Kendi is quite candid in *How to Be an Antiracist* (2019) when he states, "The only remedy to racist discrimination is antiracist discrimination. The only remedy to past discrimination is present discrimination. The only remedy to present discrimination is future discrimination."[56]

Of course, the position of US civil rights law is somewhat different. Title II of the 1964 Civil Rights Act[57] states that, "*All persons* shall be entitled to the full and equal enjoyment of the goods, services, facilities, and privileges, advantages, and accommodations of any place of public accommodation . . . *without discrimination* or segregation on the ground of race, color, religion, or national origin" (italics added). In terms of employment, Section 703 of the same act states, that "it shall be an unlawful employment practice for an employer:

- to fail or refuse to hire or to discharge any individual, or otherwise to discriminate against any individual with respect to his compensation, terms, conditions, or privileges of employment;

- to limit, segregate, or classify his employees in any way which would deprive or tend to deprive any individual of employment opportunities or otherwise adversely affect his status as an employee;

- to fail or refuse to refer for employment, or otherwise to discriminate against, any individual because of his race, color, religion, sex, or national origin, or to classify or refer for employment any individual on the basis of his race, color, religion, sex, or national origin."

Finally, the 1972 Education Amendments to the Civil Rights Act of 1964 state that "no person in the United States shall," "on the ground of race, color, or national origin," (Title VI[58]) or "on the basis of sex," (Title IX[59]) "be subjected to discrimination under any program or activity receiving federal financial assistance."

Kendi's statement is perhaps illustrative of why many CRT apologists are less forthright in their public statements. The obvious irreconcilability of CRT and civil rights law cannot have escaped the attention of CRT's *legal* defenders. Likewise, CRT's defenders in the press are likely to understand that an *informed* American public will not support racism masquerading as antiracism.

Americans who believe in the civil rights tradition and in equality before the law must stand together to resist and topple CRT and the undeserved moral authority it has usurped. In chapters 7 and 8, we provide strategies and concrete suggestions for fighting back.

STUDY QUESTIONS

1. How does CRT conflict with the civil rights movement?

2. What laws and amendments do CRT practices violate?

3. How do CRT proponents respond to anti-CRT claims?

4. Why do CRT proponents' responses not withstand scrutiny?

CHAPTER 7

Strategies for Resisting Critical Race Theory's Influence

SURVEYING THE BATTLEFIELD

CRT FIRST SECURED A BASE OF SUPPORT IN AMERICAN UNIVERSITIES AND THEN proceeded to infiltrate the remaining major institutions of American society. As CRT opponents, our objective must be to arrest CRT's momentum and then to drive it out of "the real world" and back into academic obscurity. In formulating strategies to this effect, we start with a frank assessment of the battlefield: the terrain, actors, and resources (including will).

Cultural Marxism's "long march through the institutions" is nearly complete. CRT now permeates the political and administrative arms of the government, the news media, the academy, entertainment, and the arts. Excepting for political government, which changes hands regularly, these institutions have been, broadly speaking, "left-leaning" for some time. Here, CRT's advance seems relatively straightforward: The preferences of left-leaning Americans shape left-leaning institutions and vice versa. CRT's presence in the academy and in media[1] reinforce one another and drive the leftward radicalization of (particularly, white) liberals on racial issues (aka, "the Great Awokening").[2] This process is further compounded by online "echo chambers"[3] and by social media.[4]

CRT's rapid advance through, broadly speaking, "conservative" institutions is proceeding along several paths; however, it is worth pausing here to acknowledge how profoundly conservatives underestimated the vulnerability of "their" institutions. Until recently, the idea of churches, the military, and business cozying up en masse to a movement opposed to Christianity, America, and capitalism seemed unthinkable.[5] If indeed "the facts of life are conservative," as Margaret Thatcher assured us,[6] the normal course of things (e.g., getting a job, starting a family) should have provided the antidote to campus-style radicalism.

In the case of the military, CRT indoctrination is well underway, and the key vulnerability appears to be the institution's exposure to politics.[7] The Biden Administration is actively punishing CRT-objecting service members[8] all the while "waving the bloody shirt" of the Capitol Hill riot to purge the military of so-called "extremists."[9] As evidenced by the recent campaign to exclude conservative National Guardsmen from the inauguration,[10] "extremism" is code for "Trump support." Indeed, it seems broader than this. Under the leadership of a CRT zealot,[11] the Pentagon's Countering Extremism Working Group is busy creating new categories of extremists. Among the recent additions, "patriot extremists" are those said to harbor dangerous beliefs, including notions that the US government

- has become corrupt, or
- has overstepped its constitutional boundaries, or
- is no longer capable of protecting the people against foreign threats.

Of course, such beliefs aren't even remotely extreme. Allegations of corruption are commonplace in American politics. Point 2 has been a consensus view among Republicans since the New Deal; a 2019 Gallup poll found that 56 percent of Americans believe that the government has too much power.[12] Point 3 is similarly mundane. Is no one permitted to question the government's aptitude in combatting terrorism, or foreign pathogens, or drug smuggling by foreign cartels, or election interference (from Russians, that is)?

Even more absurd than preventing young patriots from serving their country on such grounds is the notion that CRT has any place in the armed forces to begin with. CRT claims the basis for systemic racism and white supremacy resides in the nation's DNA through the Constitution. American servicemen and -women swear oaths of allegiance to that same Constitution and defend the country with their lives.[13] Every one of them is therefore a white supremacist, according to CRT.

Several distinct causes are apparent regarding CRT's e: churches. The first mirrors the path taken by CRT in left-le: tions—i.e., through church members. This is because many churches are, in fact, left-leaning institutions. Mainline Protestantism, for example, has been fairly "liberal" for some time, especially due to the influence of the "social gospel."[14] Second, CRT's institutional hegemony establishes its respectability among the "right sort of people," those that elites want to be or to be *seen* as being.[15] Institution leaders (e.g., pastors, senior managers, CEOs) might be susceptible to this kind of values-based status-signaling. Third, as noted, Christianity created a moral revolution in terms of how society perceives the dignity and value of the vulnerable and the oppressed.[16] Christianity profoundly shapes the larger cultural environment in which Marxist perspectives find resonance. In this sense, the church is inherently vulnerable to CRT.

Of the three besieged conservative institutions, CRT's business foothold—aka "Woke Capital"—is the most cynically self-interested. To be sure, the changing preferences of liberal employees and activist HR departments[17] impact business culture in ways exogenous to leadership. At the same time, company leaders are choosing to embrace social justice causes rejected by their own consumers (e.g., ESPN),[18] to aggressively push fringe and unpopular[19] policies (e.g., Delta Airlines),[20] and of course, to belittle their own employees (e.g., Coca-Cola).[21] The question is why? More precisely, given that the business of business is making money, why have major American corporations concluded that embracing CRT is profitable?

Results from a recent survey experiment published by the *Harvard Business Review* (HBR) shed light on this question. HBR researchers surveyed attitudes toward a fictitious company.[22] They informed participants that the company was either "liberal" or "conservative" in terms of the public causes it supports and in terms of the personal values of its CEO. The conservative company was rated 33 percent less favorably by participants, and this difference was *entirely* attributable to negative evaluations by self-identified Democrats. Republicans were not swayed one way or the other by the company's political stance.

This asymmetry is visible as well in party politics where Democrats routinely press business[23] to advance liberal policies while Republicans defend business's right to be unencumbered by politics and by government, generally.[24] Conservatives also lag liberals in terms of political contributions and participation (e.g., volunteering and protesting). Richard Hanania frames this discrepancy in terms of "ordinal" and "cardinal" utility.[25] A voter expresses his/her perceptions of ordinal utility in choosing Candidate A over Candidate B. The intensity of this preference (cardinal utility) is irrelevant insofar as each voter votes only once. Outside of elections, however, liberals' dramatic advantage over conservatives in terms of cardinal utility pressures institutions to bend left. The difference between the two groups might be partly dispositional, but ideology is undoubtedly a major factor.[26]

The business community has taken note that one side of the political divide "gives away the milk for free" while the other demands, "buy the milk, or else:" "*plata o plomo*," as Pablo Escobar would say. American industry is consequently repaying the voters who delivered them corporate tax cuts and deregulation with CRT workforce indoctrination and public denunciations of systemic racism. There is a valuable lesson to be learned here: the bottom line has no loyalty.

A final note on institutions: in 1989, John O'Sullivan observed that institutions drift "leftward" over time.[27] He included as examples the NAACP and Amnesty International, both of which were formerly associated with prominent conservatives. O'Sullivan speculated that the people who staff institutions generally don't like "right-wing things" like "private profit," "business," and the social order, though he suggested that "explicitly conservative" institutions were immune from this trend. With the benefit of hindsight, it is clear that "O'Sullivan's First Law" was far too modest: explicitly conservative institutions—e.g., Fox News,[28] the Drudge Report,[29] and Christian colleges[30]—as well as private industry have all shifted markedly left.

The cause of leftward institutional drift is somewhat opaque. Kevin Williamson suggests that hiring managers typically hire other people like themselves.[31] This seems reasonable. One can imagine additional factors, among them, size. Institutions typically grow over time and, in the case of business, size is accompanied with government entanglement, including opportunities for "rent-seeking."[32] As Bill Gates might attest, "playing ball" with the government is often the safest bet.[33]

Institutional leftward drift is important, but not because "the Left" and CRT are synonymous. They are not.[34] It is rather that culturally liberal institutions seem to be more susceptible to CRT influence operating through the preferences of liberal managers and workers.

Having appraised the lay of the land, we offer the following strategic frames to help CRT opponents develop resistance tactics:

1. CRT's institutional dominance means that CRT opponents are "insurgents." It is a common refrain for nonradicals (not just conservatives) to speak of themselves in terms like "ordinary people," "real America" and "the silent majority." CRT opponents might outnumber proponents,[35] but their influence sorely lags their numbers. CRT opponents must, therefore, adopt an "underdog" mentality and work hard to enhance the cardinal preferences of their troops—get people mobilized, in other words.

2. Most institutions will have to be recaptured because the country cannot do without them. At the same time, war is an economy. In some cases, it will be more effective to degrade and dismantle an institution than to recapture it.

3. Leftward institutional drift seems to be a kind of natural law. Enhancing economic dynamism—increasing the number of rising and falling companies—might help impede the overall leftward drift of economic institutions. Actively breaking up concentrations of economic power, particularly those in the hands of CRT proponents, should be on the table.[36]

4. CRT's proponents are clearly committed. Are we? More specifically, are you? Are you willing to match the other side's zeal when it comes to pressuring the institutions? There are limits, of course. We can't oppose free speech rights for CRT advocates, for example, but to foreshadow policy proposals to come, must we reimburse education loans to support racist and anti-American college instruction? Winning this fight will require us to step out of our comfort zones.

5. Establishment or "movement" conservatism is now *well past* its sell-by date. To reiterate, not every CRT opponent is a conservative (more on this below), but conservatives are and will continue to be pivotal in this fight. Reagan-era conservatism coalesced in response to the challenges of a different era. A new fusionism is now needed, something likewise tethered to conservative philosophy but adapted for the tasks at hand.

6. Even so, the conflict with CRT will test conservatism's limits because there are important philosophical tensions to consider. First, going back to Edmund Burke (1789), conservatism views institutions as key sources of social stability.[37] With the dramatic advance of CRT, the institutions are now key sources of *in*stability. Fighting within and against institutions will be awkward, particularly for conservative intellectuals. Second, the fight against CRT pits "the people" against "the elites," but populism and conservatism are awkward bedfellows. Conservatism understands that society is inherently hierarchical and that opposing elites *per se* doesn't make sense.[38] Conservatives instead seek *good* elites: those who will put the well-being of their country and people first. To the extent that American elites embrace CRT, they reject the country they lead. Even the French aristocracy, for all its faults, wasn't anti-France. Populism and conservatism are therefore united of necessity, but the tension will have to be managed.

JOINING THE BATTLE: "VOICE"

With this in mind, we offer a final framework by which to evaluate our CRT resistance efforts: voice, exit, and guerilla warfare. In Exit, Voice, and Loyalty (1970), Albert Hirschman proposes that, faced with unsatisfactory circumstances, members of organizations (nations, businesses, etc.) have two options: they can attempt to change circumstances by voicing their grievances or they can exit the organization. We figuratively add "guerrilla warfare" to this framework, drawing on Rosemary O'Leary's work highlighting efforts by rogue public servants to undermine government agencies from within.[39]

Viewed in this light, most current and potential CRT resistance efforts fall under "voice." Political scientist David Mayhew (1974) famously proposed that members of Congress should be viewed as "single-minded seekers of reelection."[40] Mayhew's claim is overstated but insightful. Obtaining reelection is not sufficient for most members of Congress (they have other goals) but it is, without question, necessary. Your federal, state, and local representatives care what you think; or rather, they *will* care, if they are persuaded that their continued employment depends on addressing your concerns.

Through the use of "voice," several important efforts have been made to counteract CRT's growing influence in America's civic and political life. President Trump's now-rescinded executive order was one; since then, state governments have passed similar restrictions. As discussed in chapter 6, legal challenges to CRT are underway. Certainly, much ink has been spilled on the subject of CRT in books, news and (a few) journal articles, op-eds, and indeed, this book. A few prominent voices in the media—including influential liberal voices—are speaking out against CRT as expressed in cancel culture.[41] By far, the most exciting development has been the engagement of the American public.[42] Public mobilization emboldens CRT's skeptics in institutions (including the government) and signals to those who are unsure, or just indifferent, the direction in which the wind is blowing. Mobilization is essential.

A note for conservatives: recent events demonstrate that prominent GOP elected officials continue to prioritize donors ahead of voters.[43] Party leaders are signaling that they expect voters to support them regardless of what they do in office. Convince them otherwise through your emails, phone calls, letters to newspaper editors, and support for their primary opponents. One especially powerful way to impact GOP politics is by becoming a precinct committeeman, where you can help to choose party leaders from "the inside."[44]

A note for liberals: if you are concerned about the onward march of this fundamentally illiberal ideology, don't be shy. Let your legislators (federal, state, and local), friends, and colleagues know that they aren't alone. Remind them that freedom of speech, equal treatment under law, and rational inquiry are all liberal values and that the Constitution is, in many ways, a liberal document. CRT and its associated "woke culture" have their prominent left-wing critics[45] and ample grounds for criticism from the Left.[46] The American Left needs more of these voices and the country needs a broad-based, bipartisan "coalition of the unwoke" to defeat this movement.[47] CRT proponents like to claim that silence is "complicity" or "violence."[48] Those of us—left, right, and center—whose worldview is grounded in the American tradition need not resort to such bullying tactics; rather, we can simply say that "courage is contagious."

Letting our voices be heard is not exclusively a matter of politics. All the institutions must be engaged. Companies need to know that consumers won't stand for workplace CRT indoctrination or for CRT-inspired public rhetoric. Let companies like Nike know that they can *either* promote public figures such as Colin Kaepernick who condemn the 4th of July as a "celebration of white supremacy" *or* they can have your business.[49] Disney recently learned this lesson the hard way.[50] Ultimately, if "voice" fails—i.e., if the institutions fail to adjust to our expressed concerns—other options are available.

JOINING THE BATTLE: "EXIT"

When institutions refuse to budge, we can still influence them simply by leaving. We can think of using "exit" to undermine hostile, CRT-held institutions by removing our resources from them—our approval, time, money, and/or viewership (i.e., ad revenues, so also money).

We can also think of *displacing* hostile institutions as an extension of exit. You can, for example, quit Facebook, Twitter, YouTube, and other censorious tech platforms and join alternative platforms like CloutHub, Parler, Gab, Rumble, and others.[51] Doing so hits the hostile institution twice, much as a disaffected voter costs his/her party two votes: one from the withdrawal of support and another from handing that support to the opposition. The downside of leaving is that we remove our voices from influencing large public spaces. It is worth thinking carefully about when to abandon mainstream platforms and when to remain; however, there does not seem to be any downside to giving patronage to their competitors.

It is also important to emphasize that exit should not be viewed merely as a defensive tactic. The point can be illustrated using Rod Dreher's *Benedict Option* (2017).[52] Writing for a conservative Christian audience, Dreher proposes a strategic withdrawal from mainstream society and culture into "intentional communities of countercultural witness"—i.e., likeminded people living apart from the dominant culture according to their own values.

Dreher is sometimes mischaracterized as advocating something like a retreat to the hills while the cities (institutions) burn in preparation for a reseeding of civilization in the rubble at some later date. Such an approach to exit would be exclusively defensive, making no attempt to impact the larger world languishing beyond the monastery's walls. The obvious problem with this approach is that CRT permits no quarter from its reach.

What Dreher actually advocates is strategic withdrawal coupled with active efforts (offense) to impact the dominant culture from a renewed position of strength. He incorporates the idea of a "parallel polis," from the Czech anti-communist Václav Benda; roughly, an alternative society—network of institutions and culture—cohabiting the same space as the dominant society and drawing in emigrants from that society. As Dreher states:

The parallel polis is not about building a gated community for Christians but rather about establishing (or re-establishing) common practices and common institutions that can reverse the isolation and fragmentation of contemporary society. (In this we hear Brother Ignatius of Norcia's call to have "borders"—formal lines behind which we live to nurture our faith and culture—but to *push outwards, infinitely*") (italics added).[53]

Adapting this approach to resisting CRT in our private lives, we can think of homeschooling networks and private schools (including excellent "classical schools")[54] as alternative institutions in a parallel, unwoke polis. We can remove ourselves from streaming services that push CRT distortions[55] and other reprehensible content[56] by creating and patronizing alternative streaming platforms. The *Daily Wire* is leading the way in this regard, venturing into entertainment with movies such as *Run, Hide, Fight*[57] and novels like *Another Kingdom*.[58]

Companies can likewise use exit to take a stand against CRT. We describe a powerful method for doing so in the following chapter; however, briefly, companies can replace divisive DEI training regimes with alternative approaches to workforce diversity management that enhance employee cooperation and unity. Recall that such approaches strike not one but two blows against CRT. Businesses can also help to mitigate thought and speech control imposed by CRT advocates by hiring the victims of cancel culture, as demonstrated by the *Daily Wire* when it effectively uncancelled actress Gina Carano.[59] Business can also help to "cancel the cancellers," as Idaho internet provider Your T1 WIFI demonstrated when it blocked Facebook and Twitter in response to the social media platforms blocking President Trump.[60]

JOINING THE BATTLE: "GUERRILLA WARFARE"

CRT's institutional dominance means that its opponents must learn to think more like *insurgents*. For inspiration as to what an insurgent mentality looks like in practice, we look back to the original counterculture. In his 1971 *Rules for Radicals*, Saul Alinsky encourages revolutionaries to infiltrate mainstream institutions while keeping their views hidden.[61] Only once in positions of power should their aims become evident. Clearly someone was paying attention!

Such an approach is plainly neither "voice" nor "exit." As noted, we propose these three frames for readers to consider on a case-by-case basis. Presumably, quitting your job ("exit") over your company's CRT posture is not feasible. You might also want to avoid voicing your objections to CRT during the hiring process. This isn't "infiltration" so much as "common sense" but the point here is to act effectively as circumstances allow. In this context, "guerrilla warfare"—our broad, catch-all category for "irregular tactics"—is a third method we can use to resist CRT.

Consider the weaponization of humor and, specifically, of ridicule. Per Alinsky, "ridicule is man's most potent weapon. There is no defense. It is almost impossible to counterattack ridicule. Also, it infuriates the opposition, who then react to your advantage."[62] Ridicule is particularly powerful when it is directed against dominant or "hegemonic" norms and values. This is because the dominance of these norms depends on the public respect they command. Ridicule *was* a potent weapon for radicals when they were on "the outside," in the counterculture. Having all but won their cultural revolution, opponents of radicalism are the new counterculture. Ridicule is now among our most potent weapons.

This is the context in which we approach online "trolling" campaigns and political meme culture. Consider a few such examples targeting the mainstream news media:

- For decades, the conventional wisdom held that people negatively impacted by globalization should adjust to resulting job losses and limited employment prospects by simply retooling their own skillsets. One stand-in for this view was the phrase "learn to code." Opponents of globalization considered "learn to code" to be an elitist "let them eat cake" kind of response to what was, in their view, a series of government policy-driven changes to the structure of the American economy. Consequently, in 2019, when many journalists—i.e., former enthusiastic propagators of this conventional wisdom—faced a severely worsening job market, their critics tweeted to them "learn to code."[63]

- Members of the group QAnon believe, among other things, that the US government is run by a secret cabal of Satan-worshipping pedophiles who manage a global sex-trafficking ring. They further believe that President Trump was recruited by the military to expose this cabal and to bring it to justice.[64] It is a strange movement, to put it mildly. It is also a *very pro-Trump* movement, as one might expect— i.e., if the choice is between Trump on the one hand and Satanist pedophiles on the other!

Left-leaning media pundits have responded by associating Republicans and conservative viewpoints with QAnon,[65] and by working to delegitimize conservative views as "conspiracy theories."[66] In response, some conservative activists embraced the term "Blue Anon" as a stand-in for, as they see it, discredited liberal conspiracies like the Russia collusion investigation, the Jussie Smollett hate crime hoax, the Covington Catholic kids scandal, and the idea that the US government is presently under threat from a right-wing insurgency.[67]

- Finally, in response to perceptions of widespread, reflexive press hostility toward President Trump, his supporters created the NPC meme. In video games, an NPC refers to a "non-player character."[68] NPCs engage with players in limited, formulaic fashions; for example, repeating the same lines. In the NPC meme, journalists repeat the phrase "Orange man bad" in unison because they, like a simple video game character, lack the ability to engage with players (the public) in greater depth.

In each case, guerrilla tactics ridicule dominant institutions and so assault their legitimacy. "Learn to code" and "Blue Anon" accuse the institution of hypocrisy. "Learn to code" demands that dominant actors live by their own standards—another Alinsky tactic.[69] "Blue Anon" takes aim at the press as an authority on matters of fact and fiction—its very *raison d'etre*. The NPC meme highlights media bias, impartiality being (believe it or not!) another key source of news media legitimacy. As if to prove Alinsky's observative, Twitter banned "learn to code" and the NPC meme, allegedly to safeguard its users.[70] Doing so only compounds the damage by demonstrating the vulnerability of the dominant paradigm to childish criticism, not that trust in media is high to begin with.[71] After Blue Anon was removed from the *Urban Dictionary* and censored from internet searches by Google, the term became a top trender on Twitter.[72]

In terms of guerilla tactics more directly relevant to CRT, consider the "white saviors" meme constructed from the popular show *Game of Thrones* (GOT).[73] The "white savior complex" is yet another indictment leveled at white people by "woke" antiracists. The claim is that whites often ostentatiously help people of color to aggrandize themselves. The white savior GOT meme flips this accusation back onto the (white) CRT proponent, accusing them of grandstanding and, implicitly, of hypocrisy.[74] The picture depicts the white savior (Daenerys Targaryen) surrounded by a sea of dark-skinned worshipers. The caption reads, "How white people see themselves when they post anti-white posts." This meme is hard-hitting, salient, and above all, funny. Wherever possible, we should be happy warriors!

At the same time, there are some definite perils to avoid when using guerilla tactics to combat CRT. Certainly, the online meme world has its share of people and content (e.g., the Alt Right) that would tar our resistance movement by association. CRT proponents will endeavor to draw such connections wherever possible, and there is no reason for us to make it easy for them to do so. As opponents of Critical Race Theory, we are opponents of racism; not of "racism" as absurdly reimagined by CRT, but of actual racism: of hating and/or believing people to be superior/inferior based on their race. We must hold to our own standards even while demolishing those of our opponents.

Don't despair if these strategies seem a bit too complicated. Our next chapter presents ten concrete recommendations that offer a multipronged attack on CRT's radical agenda. We are encouraged that the battle is winnable and that Americans are standing up and fighting back in a bold and efficacious manner.

STUDY QUESTIONS

1. What institutions has CRT influenced?

2. Why do businesses embrace CRT?

3. What considerations are important in developing resistance tactics?

4. How does the framework "voice, exit, and guerilla warfare" relate to fighting back against CRT?

CHAPTER 8

Fighting Back

THIS BOOK IS ALL ABOUT ACTION. IT IS A CALL FOR THE "WE THE PEOPLE" addressed in the preamble of the U.S. Constitution to "Be the People" who take a stand for the guiding principles that have undergirded our nation and made it the envy of the world. Our goal has been to inform you about CRT, a dangerous ideology that has indoctrinated millions of Americans and taken over many of our institutions. In this final chapter we provide an action plan for combatting CRT. Several of the proposals we list speak to public policy and call for your support in terms of your advocacy, volunteerism, and/or contributions—whatever you can reasonably do. Politics and public policy have the greatest potential to influence every other institution of American society. Policy is where CRT can inflict the most damage, and so it is where we must concentrate much of our resistance efforts. At the same time, there is a world beyond politics that is likewise under siege. We therefore include suggestions for how you can resist CRT in your personal life and help to construct a culture where others can do the same.

We list our ten proposals below for quick reference and then explain them in greater detail in the following section. We conclude this chapter and book with a list of resources you can use to learn more about CRT in theory and in practice, and where you can go to find allies in this fight.

TEN PROPOSALS FOR RESISTING CRT

1. Continue to research what CRT is, where it comes from, how it impacts American society, and how to combat its influence.

2. Challenge the legality and constitutionality of CRT in education and in the workplace.

3. Organize grassroots movements to elect school boards, city council members, and mayors to eliminate CRT and related indoctrination efforts (e.g., 1619 curriculums) within their respective domains.

4. Build broad coalitions stretching across racial, ethnic, and partisan divides.

5. Use multiple strategies, including town hall meetings, writing op-eds, contacting public officials, and organizing rallies, to share information about the harm caused by CRT to children and to others.

6. Educate church leaders and encourage them to lead on racial issues using principles of biblical justice.

7. Bring pressure to bear on corporations and other institutions that support CRT.

8. Stand up to Big Tech companies that seek to limit political speech.

9. Monitor state and local agencies to ensure that taxpayers are not subsidizing organizations that advance hostility to America and to American values.

10. Develop alternatives to diversity, equity, and inclusion (DEI) training.

APPLYING THE PROPOSALS

1. Understanding CRT

We think that the most important contribution this book makes is in emphasizing strategies and tactics for resisting CRT in practice. At the same time, we have discussed what we believe are the most essential aspects of CRT because we want you to know your enemy, to paraphrase Sun Tzu (credited as the author of the classic work *The Art of War*). Of course, much more has been written on this subject, and we encourage you to avail yourself of as many resources as you can. We list many such resources in Appendix A; however, briefly, readers who are interested in other scholarly accounts should consider *Cynical Theories* (2020) by Helen Pluckrose and James Lindsay.[1] Readers interested in Critical Race Theory's penetration of Christianity and of the military should consider *Fault Lines* (2021) by Voddie Baucham[2] and *Irresistible Revolution* (2021) by Matthew Lohmeier.[3] These last two are recent books written by a Christian minister and a former Space Force Commander, respectively. For online resources, we recommend "Critical Race Theory, the New Intolerance, and Its Grip on America" by Butcher and Gonzalez (2020)[4] and the New Discourses "Social Justice Encyclopedia"[5] for comprehensive accounts of CRT in theory. For accounts of CRT in practice, we encourage readers to peruse Christopher Rufo's considerable work[6] as well as his "CRT Legislation Tracker."[7]

2. Challenging CRT under law

As discussed in chapter 6, parents, students, employees, and citizen activists are taking a stand by challenging CRT's implementation on legal and constitutional grounds. We share the concerns of CRT's legal critics that CRT instruction in K-12 schools and in workforce DEI training violates First and Fourteenth Amendment protections as well as civil rights law.[8] It should be emphasized that this conflict is *fundamental*—it is not a "technical" matter that CRT proponents can "tweak" to save CRT instruction in practice. If courts remove from CRT instruction racial harassment[9] and discrimination,[10] hostile learning[11] and working environments,[12] compelled confessions of racial guilt,[13] retribution for non-compliance,[14] and racial segregation,[15] what remains would not be "CRT" in any meaningful sense.

You can help these efforts by gathering and publicizing evidence (e.g., school curricula, policy memoranda, training documents, etc.) of abusive CRT practices. You can pass information along to organizations such as No Left Turn in Education[16] and to other leaders in this fight. You can also take legal action yourself if you feel that your rights have been violated. We also recommend for your reading a letter to and legal response from the Secretary of State of Montana that stopped CRT in its tracks.[17]

3. Building grassroots resistance movements

Across the nation, parents are mobilizing and taking decisive action to remove CRT from school curricula.[18] Recently, in Southlake, Texas, CRT opponents secured a landslide local election victory.[19] At the time of this writing, statewide CRT curriculum bans have been proposed in eleven states[20] and passed in four: Tennessee,[21] Oklahoma,[22] Iowa,[23] and Idaho.[24] In Appendix B, we include a model school board CRT ban provided by *Citizens for Renewing America*.[25] This is something tangible that you can personally take to your school board to put an end to CRT indoctrination in schools in your community!

This is representative government at its best: popular mobilization driving institutional change. We need to ramp up the pressure. We need more grassroots groups, more petitions, more phone calls, emails, and letters to politicians and school administrators, more active school board involvement,[26] more protests, all of it. We have forty-six states to go.

An important aside is that such efforts are not (and should not be) prohibitions of discussing slavery, Jim Crow, or other examples of where the United States has failed to live up to its ideals.[27] A proper education in American history requires learning and discussing such facts. Simply put, CRT is a matter of narrative, not of fact. CRT is a story about America, one that is explicitly hostile to American identity and values. Other stories (perspectives) on American history and society could include:

- the white supremacist perspective
- the monarchist perspective
- the government-is-run-by-lizard-people perspective.

Excluding inaccurate and divisive narratives does not limit the free speech rights of students or teachers. As Rufo notes, the specific language of CRT bans—prohibiting "race essentialism, collective guilt, and racial superiority theory"—would prevent racist instruction of any kind (monarchist and lizard-people narratives remain untouched, however).[28] As parents and citizens invested in our country's future, we have a responsibility to ensure that school curricula are accurate and that they serve the public interest by helping to mold future citizens capable of sustaining a free society.

To this end, we should set up "1776 mini-Commissions" at the state and local levels. Such commissions would mirror efforts by the previous 1776 Commission[29] and by the Woodson Center's 1776 Unites[30] to replace divisive and inaccurate 1619-inspired curricula with a curriculum that is accurate, patriotic, and racially unifying. Such curricula should emphasize America's true founding principles (and date: 1776!) as well as successes achieved and contributions made by Americans of all backgrounds to our shared history, society, and culture. We should also look to K-12 school districts around the country for examples of excellent curricula we can model and replicate.

4. Building broad coalitions

We need a mass movement of resistance to overcome CRT's stranglehold on institutions. We need to organize parents and other concerned citizens, speak out in public forums, contact public officials, pressure candidates, hold rallies, and generally create the impression (and reality) of an overwhelming movement. To this end, we should view ourselves as partisans of the American tradition and set aside other disputes. The broader and more diverse—politically, racially, etc.—our movement is, the more effective it will be. This is particularly true where racial diversity is concerned. It is a simple fact that CRT's premises render it especially vulnerable to criticism from racial minorities and, in particular, to criticism from the eternal victims in the CRT worldview: black Americans.

5. Getting the word out

Defeating CRT demands an "all hands on deck" approach. We inform ourselves first (Proposal 1), and then we inform others. We can do the latter using op-eds and letters to the editor, and we can share our views with friends and colleagues, including on social media. Letters to public officials, rallies, and town hall engagement all magnify our message and signal strength: numbers and commitment. Such efforts are beginning to show signs of success.[31]

As we work to spread the word about CRT, it might be most effective to emphasize what CRT looks like in *practice*. CRT's strength is that it preys on people's empathy for the downtrodden and for the disadvantaged (though, ironically, CRT diminishes empathy by circumscribing it to favored groups[32]). Understanding CRT's premises and origins takes time—not that we have to tell *you* this in the final chapter of this book!—but a deep dive into theory is not required for most people to understand why, for example, it is both unjust and cruel to force small children to feel shame for their racial identity and for historical injustices over which they had no control. To justify CRT in practice, one needs either a very hard heart or a considerable deprogramming of one's natural moral instincts.

6. Engaging the churches

America's largest Protestant denomination, the Southern Baptist Church (SBC), is presently embroiled in a controversy[33] stemming from a 2019 resolution[34] bringing CRT into the church. Similar splits exist elsewhere in the Christian church[35]; however, the SBC case is especially striking in that the two sides seemingly agree on questions of doctrine, moral traditionalism, and even on the question of CRT's anti-Christian foundations. The split over CRT is rather an extension of the nation's racial divide. That any orthodox and informed Christian could view CRT positively speaks to the depth of this wound.

CRT's proponents in the church are rightly focused on confronting racism; however, supplanting Christianity with Marxism is plainly wrong. By any decent measure, the "woke church" is an abomination. Christianity provides a firm foundation for viewing one another as equals and for treating each other with love and dignity. It provides no foundation for viewing one another as natural enemies or for retribution against entire groups in the name of "social justice." The fact that so many Christians failed to see the *Imago Dei* in their fellow man in the past does not excuse, much less necessitate, repeating this failure in the present. Use your knowledge to help church leaders remove CRT's divisive rhetoric from their congregations.

7. Confronting woke institutions

President Trump's now-rescinded ban[36] on CRT training in federal agencies should be reinstated and state governments should follow his lead, as Arkansas already has.[37] We need much more action on this front.[38] At all levels of government, we should be pushing for changes to fiscal and regulatory policy to make life more difficult for companies who push CRT on their employees and easier for those who do not. Tax shelters for foundations and nonprofits that fund CRT should be scrapped. Employee civil rights protections should be aggressively enforced and, indeed, extended to encourage employees to sue companies for subjecting them to DEI workforce training. If there are additional grounds on which to target CRT companies—anticompetitive practices, for example—we should pursue those as well.

In addition, we believe that no compelling public interest is served by instructing young Americans to hate their country and their fellow citizens. As such, we can think of no reason for government to continue to subsidize CRT college instruction through grants and loans. Obviously, students should be free to take whatever course they are willing to pay for themselves. Policymakers should also consider the academic and broader societal merits of related, heavily Marxism-influenced fields. Certainly, degrees in CRT and perhaps, in related fields, should be delisted from fulfilling education requirements for government hiring purposes.

Moving beyond public policy, we can incorporate the principles of "voice, exit, and guerrilla warfare" described in the previous chapter into our efforts to dissuade major institutions from pushing CRT. Briefly, you can "voice" your objections to CRT public rhetoric and to DEI training. If, for example, you are a major stockholder or supplier to a "woke" business, or even if you are just a *consumer* of business products (we all are), you have leverage. If the institution fails to relent, you can exert additional pressure by depriving it of your resources ("exit"): your money, your time, etc. Finally, we can think of nonvoice/exit approaches to combating CRT in the institutions as (figurative) "guerrilla warfare" tactics: e.g., working to undermine the legitimacy of CRT-promoting institutions.

8. Standing Up to Big Tech

In terms of "woke institutions," America's dominant technology companies and social media platforms ("Big Tech") deserve special consideration. The problem is not merely that these major companies, like so many others, have embraced CRT—e.g., Twitter CEO Jack Dorsey donated $10 billion to Ibram X. Kendi's Center for Antiracist Research[39]—rather, it is that they routinely leverage their monopoly control to mandate the CRT worldview by excluding dissenting voices from the nation's "digital commons." Examples of Big Tech censorship and other abusive practices include:

- blocking, banning, shadow banning, and demonetizing users expressing disfavored views,[40]

- shielding favored viewpoints, groups, and individuals from criticism,[41]

- ignoring some kinds of "hate speech," threats, and other abusive practices (e.g., doxing), even by their own standards,[42]

- interfering in US elections by censoring important news stories[43] and by deplatforming[44] candidates, as well as the former president,[45] and

- defending such actions by suggesting that critics form their own platforms while simultaneously coordinating to sabotage such platforms.

Thankfully, Florida is leading the way in reining in these abusive and discriminatory practices[46] and other states are following suit.[47] Policy makers should consider adding political viewpoint discrimination to existing civil rights protections. Ultimately, Section 230 of the Communications Decency Act must be altered or repealed at the federal level. As elsewhere, your advocacy is needed here.

9. Monitoring state and local agencies to ensure that taxpayers are not subsidizing organizations that advance hostility to America and to American values

There are many ways you can monitor state and local government agencies in your area. Check your local city and county websites for committee meeting minutes, agendas, and dates; attend those meetings when practicable. For information not available online, you can submit a Freedom of Information Act (FOIA) request at your local government's office. The National Conference of State Legislatures offers searchable databases[48] that allow you to watch for pending legislation in areas that CRT can affect, like education. These and other resources will help you stay abreast of any attempts to use taxpayer dollars to support CRT.

10. Developing alternatives to Diversity, Equity, and Inclusion training programs

We believe CRT has metastasized in the workplace because it addresses a real need; namely, that companies have diverse workforces. In general, diversity (difference) is an asset to companies in that it brings additional perspectives to bear on tasks; however, diversity becomes a liability when those different perspectives clash in unproductive ways. In this way, diversity is like a force of nature—e.g., like fire. Harness it properly and reap the rewards. Fail to do so and get burned. We find that too many companies are being pushed into bringing in diversity trainers whose destructive messages create havoc in the workplace and leave people much worse off. Fortunately, there is an alternative.

President Biden has reversed the Trump executive orders(EO) banning CRT in federal agencies and issued several new orders of his own designed to address discrimination against marginalized groups and underserved populations.[49] Institutions face enormous pressures to take action. Instead of hiring DEI trainers steeped in CRT, we need to compete in this space before workplaces and learning environments are disrupted. It is possible to educate people about diversity and to be sensitive to the needs and contributions of others without pitting men against women, whites against blacks, and the LGBT members against heterosexuals. My beliefs motivated me to take action. I urge other entrepreneurs to do the same.

After the social and political unrest of 2020, I (Carol) created Unity Training Solutions[50] as an alternative to the plethora of DEI programs that use Critical Race Theory as their ideological framework. DEI training is layered on top of existing affirmative action programs, which are the law of the land. Recent studies show that DEI training does not achieve its lofty goals.[51] It is a billion-dollar industry that lacks monitoring and professional standards of conduct that one would expect from people who are preaching to us about how we should educate our children and run our businesses and workplaces.

Unity Training Solutions brings together diverse people who seek harmony and are willing to commit themselves to work on common goals and common visions for their institutions. Traditional American principles and old-fashioned common sense would suggest we can achieve greater harmony and success in institutions by respecting everyone's civil rights and equality under the law. We can accomplish this by rediscovering and re-embracing our nation's motto: *E. Pluribus Unum*—Out of Many, One. I believe most Americans hold a vision of diversity and inclusion that recognizes and appreciates the individuality each person brings to the environment. Justice and fairness can be obtained while respecting free speech and transparency. Indeed, the citizens of our nation share more similarities than differences. The goal of diversity training should be to help diverse people work together and respect each other without bringing unnecessary drama and distractions to workplaces and learning environments.

STAND YOUR GROUND

We now know that CRT impacts us in myriad ways, including at work and in our private lives. Part of the reason we find ourselves on our respective back feet is that too many of us fear being labeled "racist" and otherwise stigmatized by CRT proponents. When confronted by such people, you can and should stand your ground.[52] Doing so will not be easy, but it is the right thing to do. We should have the courage to take principled stances that can be persuasive and powerful. Stand up for yourself, for your children, and for others who are unfairly targeted by the "social justice" mob. Your courage will help others to do the same.

STUDY QUESTIONS

1. What ten things can you do to fight back against CRT?

2. What is one action you can take this week to begin resisting CRT's influence?

3. How can you stand your ground when others question your rejection of CRT?

Glossary

Action civics: Alternatively, "new civics"; is left-wing indoctrination and activism disguised as civic participation. Action civics directs students toward direct political participation (protesting, lobbying, etc.) in lieu of classroom civic education.[1] Proponents argue direct participation is both more effective and value neutral[2]; however, in practice, action civics causes are almost invariably progressive[3]—e.g., de-carbonizing the economy, massively redistributing wealth, intensifying identity group grievance, curtailing the free market, expanding government bureaucracy, elevating international 'norms' over American constitutional law, and disparaging our common history and ideals.[4]

Affirmative action: Policies and procedures in hiring and admissions created to remedy past discrimination based on protected characteristics, eliminate current unlawful discrimination, and prevent any such future discrimination.[5] It is most often used to create more diversity in terms of race/color and sex in a workplace or educational institution. See also:Civil rights, equal opportunity.

Ally: A member of a "privileged group" who takes "a subordinate and supportive role within a group of activists for an identity group seen as marginalized."[6]

Antifa: A loosely organized Far Left extremist group. Antifa stands for "antifascism"; the organization generally opposes fascism, nationalism, and white supremacy, frequently in violent or destructive ways. The group allegedly opposes authoritarianism as well; however, its use of violence and intimidation tactics, as well as its slogans (e.g., "Liberals get the bullet, too") demonstrates approval of authoritarianism in practice.[8] Antifa also decries capitalism and government, generally.[9]

Antiracist: Commitment to recognizing and fighting "racism" as understood by CRT proponents and fellow travelers (see "prejudice plus power"); a believer in racial equality and opponent of racial hierarchy; one who attributes cause for social problems (e.g., racial disparities) to systems of power and to politics rather than to group behavior differences. Importantly, an "antiracist" is distinct from someone claiming to be "not racist." The latter, according to CRT advocates, is a racist who is attempting to mask his/her racism.[7]

Black Lives Matter (organization): An organization founded in 2013 "to eradicate white supremacy and build local power to intervene in violence inflicted on black communities by the state and vigilantes."[10] Founded by Patrisse Cullors, Opal Tometi, and Alicia Garza, the group is radical and espouses neo-Marxist ideas.[11]

Black lives matter (slogan): The claim that the lives of black people do not currently matter as much as the lives of others in the United States (especially in the criminal justice system). The phrase is used to bring awareness to perceived systemic racism in an effort to effect change.[12]

Black nationalism: Support for "unity and political self-determination for black people, especially in the form of a separate black nation."[13] The black nationalist movement was particularly salient in the 1960s and 1970s in the United States and sought to promote a separate identity for people of black ancestry.[14]

Cisgender: A term for those whose gender identity matches their sex at birth; contrast with transgender.[15]

Civil liberties: Basic, guaranteed rights and freedoms in the United States, many of which originate from the Bill of Rights. Examples include freedom of speech, the right to a fair trial in court, and the right to vote.[16]

Civil rights: The right to be free from discrimination and unequal treatment based on protected characteristics that are specifically enumerated in law.[17] Protected characteristics include race/color, ethnicity, country of origin, religion, sex, age, and disability, among others.

Colonialism: When Country A takes control of Country B and sends settlers to occupy it for the purpose of exploiting Country B's people or natural resources.[18] In the CRT, postmodernist, and broader "social justice" contexts, colonialism refers to "white" and Western influences, including "white ways of knowing" (see reference).[19] Thus, to "decolonize" school curricula is to remove white authors and/or to "deconstruct" (see "deconstruction") their influence.[20]

Colorblindness: When a person either claims to not see race or ethnicity or does not consider them to be important factors in determining one's life experiences. For many years, a colorblind society was seen as the objective that, when reached, would indicate the end of racism in the United States.[21] According to CRT advocates, colorblindness is a form of racism as it allows whites to avoid acknowledging the importance of race and racism in their lives.[22]

Communism: A political and economic theory developed by Karl Marx. It encourages class war with the intention of creating a society where the government owns and redistributes all property.[23]

Critical Race Theory: According to proponents Richard Delgado and Jean Stefancic: "a collection of activists and scholars interested in studying and transforming the relationship among race, racism, and power... Critical Race Theory questions the very foundations of the liberal order, including equality theory, legal reasoning, Enlightenment rationalism, and neutral principles of constitutional law."[24] According to opponent James Lindsay: "the belief that racism is the organizing principle of society."[25] Critical Race Theory takes the standard Marxist framework and substitutes social groups (e.g., whites/blacks, men/women) for economic groups (bourgeois/proletariat).

Again, like Marxism, it advocates inverting the (claimed) existing power hierarchy.

Cultural competence: A common euphemisim for CRT in education. Alternatively, according to proponents, the "ability to understand, appreciate and interact with people from cultures or belief systems different from one's own."[26] It involves recognizing personal biases related to different cultures, acknowledging that people are treated differently based on their appearance or culture, educating oneself on cultural differences, and committing to take action to ensure fair treatment of people from all cultures or backgrounds.[27]

Cultural Marxism:
1. A term often used synonymously with "neo-Marxism" to describe an offshoot or variant of Marxism emphasizing culture and values above material conditions as the basis for class-based oppression in line with Antonio Gramsci's critique of Marxist orthodoxy and associated with the Frankfurt School (aka Critical Theory). Cultural Marxists aim to subvert the hegemony of traditional Western values by infiltrating and co-opting core social institutions.
2. An alleged conspiracy theory holding researchers from the Frankfurt School responsible for social change in line with their stated goals of demolishing (deconstructing) Western cultural institutions to facilitate social revolution. Critics of this "conspiracy theory" discredit the term by emphasizing its use by anti-Semites;[28] however, it should be noted that even ardent critics of neo-Marxism, Critical Theory, CRT, and company describe some conservative references to Cultural Marxism as "conspiratorial."[29]

Deconstruction: Analysis techniques derived from the postmodern philosopher Jacques Derrida, wherein concepts and categories are interrogated by contesting hierarchical "binary oppositions" (e.g., male/female, meaning/form, fact/fiction).[30] "In practice, deconstruction is a method by which meaning is either broken down or 'problematized,' specifically for the purposes of either showing meaning to be arbitrary . . . or to expose and rearrange the power dynamics believed to be carried by the ways words relate to one another."[31]

Doxing: A malicious act in which someone discovers a victim's personal information and circulates it online without his/her consent, generally leading to harassment in various forms. [32]

Educational equity: An ideology that asserts that every student should receive at least an adequate education, regardless of what it takes to provide it. [33] This might require differential treatment depending on the specific needs of a district or student. See also Equity, Equality.

Equality: Conventionally, "the fact of being equal in rights, status, advantages etc." [34] In CRT, "equality" is often described in terms of equal access to resources independent of need. It has also been described in terms of equal opportunity (see reference), and equal treatment. CRT advocates reject equality as an ideology used by oppressors to maintain their control over the oppressed and thus their position in society. [35] Often contrasted with equity.

Equal opportunity: The practice of nondiscrimination based on a person's race, sex, disability, status, etc., especially in regard to employment. [36]

Equal protection: As established by the Fifth and Fourteenth Amendments, the guarantee that the law will apply uniformly to all similar people or groups. Essentially, similarly situated people must be treated similarly under the law, and no one will be denied that protection. [37]

Equity: Distributional equality or equality of outcomes. CRT advocates pursue equity to address imbalanced or biased systems/institutions. To achieve equity, different groups might need to receive different resources or opportunities to achieve the same outcome. Often contrasted with equality, where all groups receive the same, rather than differential, treatment. [38]

Ethnomathematics: Different cultures can produce different mathematical systems and the systems may change over time. Our current system of mathematics is not universal but rather based in particular aspects of European culture. [39]

False consciousness: When the oppressed "internalize and identify with attitudes and ideology of the controlling class." [40] CRT advocates and Marxists consider false consciousness to be a way of thinking that is externally imposed by the majority or oppressor groups; it prevents minority or oppressed groups from understanding their true social and economic situation. False consciousness is what impedes the liberation of the oppressed from subjugation.[41]

Implicit bias: Negative associations (biases) that people unknowingly hold. In CRT discourse, this generally refers to unconscious stereotypes imposed on or judgments made of members of a different group. Also known as unconscious bias. Contrasted with explicit bias, which refers to obvious discrimination based on a person's characteristic(s).[42]

Inclusion: Welcoming people from all backgrounds into an organization. In CRT, true inclusion focuses on creating a safe environment for traditionally marginalized groups; at times, this involves the exclusion of people or ideas perceived as hostile to these groups.[43]

Interest convergence: Whites (or other majority groups) will only support the interest of blacks (or other minority groups) if their interests align.[44]

Intersectionality: One's experiences in the world are shaped by a convergence of characteristics or identity markers. These include race, gender, sexual orientation, socioeconomic status, etc. A person's level of power (or subjugation) in society depends on the intersection of these various characteristics, which interact in complex ways.[45]

Marginalized groups: Groups are "marginalized" by society when they are denied access to its benefits.[46]

Meritocracy: Traditionally, the idea that jobs and other benefits should be earned based on merit or ability, rather than based on some other factor, such as familial ties (nepotism).[47] For CRT proponents, this is an ideology that oppressors use to continue to deny equitable outcomes to others.[48]

Metanarrative: An attempt to explain historical events or other social or cultural phenomena. A metanarrative connects various events by using truths or values perceived as universal. Postmodernists reject metanarratives as a pernicious attempt to control thought.[49] See also Postmodernism.

Microaggression: An allegedly harmful insult, question, remark, or action related to a person's membership in a marginalized group. Microaggressions can be verbal or nonverbal and intentional or unintentional. CRT advocates posit that minorities experience microaggressions on a daily basis and that the effects of such experiences build up over time.[50]

Oppressors: Members of a supposedly dominant group (whites, men, heterosexuals, etc.) that exert influence over the lives and opportunities of others (the oppressed). This group has built institutions that support its continued use of power.[51]

Oppressed: Members of a supposedly nondominant group (blacks, women, LGBTQ+, etc.) whose lives are principally controlled by the decisions and actions of others (the oppressors).

Political correctness:
1. According to defenders, "language that avoids offending persons of various genders, races, sexual orientations, cultures, or social conditions."[52]
2. According to opponents, a method of thought and speech control that forces leftist ideological conformity.[53]

Postmodernism: A philosophical movement from the late 1960s. Postmodernists assert that there is no objective reality, reasoning, knowledge, or logic; all of these are merely constructed by society. Attempts to explain history or other aspects of the natural or social world are false and merely impose conformity on others. Postmodernist thinking informs CRT.[54]

Prejudice plus power: A definition of racism that states that only oppressors can be racist. Dominant groups have both prejudice and the power to act on that prejudice, resulting in racism, while nondominant groups (the oppressed) have little power and thus cannot be racist.[55]

Privilege: Per CRT advocates, power or other unearned benefits that people receive resulting from membership in a dominant group (whites, for example). Privilege usually results from and is maintained by intentionally designed societal structures.[56]

Safe spaces: Places where a person, or group of people, can go to be protected from exposure to "discrimination, criticism, harassment, or any other emotional or physical harm."[57]

Systemic racism: For CRT proponents, "the complex interaction of culture, policy, and institutions that holds in place" the negative outcomes for oppressed groups (and the resultant privilege of oppressor groups).[58] Essentially, different aspects of society, including laws, work together to maintain white dominance in the US.[59] Also commonly referred to as structural or institutional racism, although the definitions are not always perfectly interchangeable.

Tolerance: Conventionally, "sympathy or indulgence for beliefs or practices differing from one's own; the act of allowing something: toleration; the allowable deviation from a standard."[60] Tolerance in CRT terminology is reframed drawing on Herbert Marcuse's (1965) arguments in *A Critique of Pure Tolerance*. CRT demands absolute tolerance of any "protected class" while expressing extreme intolerance for "oppressor classes" such as whites, men, heterosexuals, etc.

Victimhood: A position of superior moral status to be mobilized in a religious-like fashion to transform social institutions and society.[61] Victimhood is also a superior (i.e., more accurate and informed) position from which to view the world.[62]

Ways of knowing: Different definitions of what knowledge is and how it is produced and transmitted by various groups. CRT proponents usually refer to traditional science and mathematics as "white ways of knowing" and superstition and storytelling as "black ways of knowing."[63]

White fragility: A term coined by Robin DiAngelo that means "the state in which even a minimum amount of racial stress becomes intolerable, triggering a range of defensive moves [in white people]."[64] Essentially, white people are comfortable with the current status quo and become immediately defensive if they feel that someone is questioning that status quo.[65]

White nationalism: Traditionally, an extreme, militant form of white supremacy that advocates for racial segregation.[66] More recently, white nationalism has been defined as "the belief that national identity should be built around white ethnicity, and that white people should therefore maintain both a demographic majority and dominance of the nation's culture and public life."[67]

White supremacy: In colloquial usage, the belief that white people are an intrinsically superior race that deserves to dominate all others.[68] CRT advocates use this term more liberally, employing it to describe "the pervasiveness, magnitude, and normalcy of white dominance and assumed superiority."[69]

Whiteness: The social construction of white identity centered around white supremacy and racist exclusion and oppression of people of color.[70]

Woke: The state of being keenly aware of racial and other injustice in society; implies both knowledge of inequities and action toward solutions.[71]

Notes

CHAPTER 1

1   1776 Unites, https://1776unites.com/

2   Adam Serwer, "Historians Clash with the 1619 Project," *The Atlantic*, December 23, 2019, https://www.theatlantic.com/ideas/archive/2019/12/historians-clash-1619-project/604093/

3   Robert L. Woodson Sr., *Red, White, and Black: Rescuing American History from Revisionists and Race Hustlers.* Nashville: Post Hill Press, 2021.

4   Helen Pluckrose and James Lindsay, *Cynical Theories: How Activist Scholarship Made Everything About Race, Gender, and Identity—And Why this Harms Everybody.* Durham, NC: Pitchstone Publishing, 2020.

5   James Lindsay, personal conversation, June 5, 2021, Leadership Program of the Rockies 2021 Annual Retreat, June 4-5, 2021, Colorado Springs, CO.

6   Carol M. Swain, "Does Progress Require Shaming and Embarrassing Our Children?" *Be the People News*, January 9, 2020, https://bethepeople-news.com/does-progress-require-shaming-and-embarrassing-children/; "Critical Race Theory and Christian Education," *Tennessee Star,* January 15, 2020, https://tennesseestar.com/2020/01/15/carol-swain-commentary-critical-race-theory-and-christian-education/; "Critical Race Theory Is Rooted in Cultural Marxism," *Be the People News*, January 22, 2020, https://bethepeoplenews.com/critical-race-theory-is-rooted-in-cultural-marxism/

7   Corrine Murdock, "Lipscomb University's Christian Scholars Conference to Host Ibram Kendi, 'How to Be Antiracist' Author, as Featured Speaker, Scrubs Website After Tennessee Star Inquiries," *Tennessee Star,* June 4, 2021, https://tennesseestar.com/2021/06/04/lipscomb-universitys-christian-scholars-conference-to-host-ibram-kendi-how-to-be-antiracist-author-as-featured-speaker-scrubs-website-after-tennessee-star-inquiries/

8   Julie Carr, "Corinne Murdock Finds Lipscomb Website Scrubbed After Inquiring about Dr. Ibram X. Kendi's Appearance at Christian Scholar Conference," *Tennessee Star*, June 5, 2021, https://tennesseestar.com/2021/06/05/corinne-murdock-finds-lipscomb-website-scrubbed-after-inquiring-about-dr-ibram-x-kendis-appearance-at-christian-scholar-conference/

9   Green Point Creative, *Your Brain on Drug Policy* [Video], YouTube, 2017, https://www.youtube.com/watch?v=AKXN6Vdr3g0

10   Erica Pinto, T*he Unequal Opportunity Race* [Video], YouTube, 2020, https://www.youtube.com/watch?v=vX_Vzl-r8NY

11   Kimberlé Crenshaw, "Mapping the Margins: Intersectionality, Identity Politics, and Violence against Women of Color," *Stanford Law Review 43*, 6: (1991), pp. 1241–1299.

12   Carol M. Swain, *The New White Nationalism in America: Its Challenge to Integration*. Cambridge: Cambridge University Press, 2002.

13   Christopher James Schorr, "White Nationalism and Its Challenge to the American Right," PhD diss., Georgetown University, 2020.

14   Swain, *The New White Nationalism in America.*

15   Eric Kaufmann, *Whiteshift: Populism, Immigration and the Future of White Majorities.* London: Penguin UK, 2018; Ashley Jardina, *White Identity Politics.* Cambridge: Cambridge University Press, 2019.

CHAPTER 2

1   Frank Newport, "In U.S., 87% Approve of Black-White Marriage, vs. 4% in 1958," *Gallup*, 2013, https://news.gallup.com/poll/163697/approve-marriage-blacks-whites.aspx

2   David A. Graham, "Really, Would You Let Your Daughter Marry a Democrat?" *The Atlantic*, September 27, 2012, https://www.theatlantic.com/politics/archive/2012/09/really-would-you-let-your-daughter-marry-a-democrat/262959/

3   John Murawski, "Critical Race Theory Is About to Face Its Day(s) in Court," *RealClearInvestigations*, April 27, 2021, https://www.realclearinvestigations.com/articles/2021/04/27/critical_race_theory_is_about_to_face_i

ts_days_in_court_774290.html; The Clark Lawsuit, n.d. *No Left Turn in Education*, https://noleftturn.us/the-clark-lawsuit/#1619384542554-a693ccf1-1f96

4   Richard Delgado and Jean Stefancic, *Critical Race Theory: An Introduction*. New York: NYU Press, 2017.

5   James Lindsay, personal conversation, June 5, 2021, Leadership Program of the Rockies 2021 Annual Retreat, June 4-5, Colorado Springs, CO.

6   Savala Trepczynski, "People of Color Learn at a Young Age That They Must Be Twice as Good. Now White People Need to Be Twice as Kind," *Time*, 2020, https://time.com/5871387/white-people-must-be-twice-as-kind/

7   Barry Latzer, "The Facts on Race, Crime, and Policing in America," *Law and Liberty*, 2012, https://lawliberty.org/the-facts-on-race-crime-and-policing-in-america/

8   Claire Miller, Emily Badger, Noelle Hurd, Ibram Kendi, Nathaniel Hendren, and Raj Chetty, "'When I See Racial Disparities, I See Racism.' Discussing Race, Gender and Mobility," *New York Times*, March 27, 2018, https://www.nytimes.com/interactive/2018/03/27/upshot/reader-questions-about-race-gender-and-mobility.html

9   Coleman Hughes, "Black American Culture and the Racial Wealth Gap," *Quillette*, July 19, 2018, https://quillette.com/2018/07/19/black-american-culture-and-the-racial-wealth-gap/

10   Federal Bureau of Prisons, "Inmate Gender," 2021, https://www.bop.gov/about/statistics/statistics_inmate_gender.jsp

11   U.S. Bureau of Labor Statistics, 2018, "Asian Women and Men Earned More Than Their White, Black, and Hispanic Counterparts in 2017," https://www.bls.gov/opub/ted/2018/asian-women-and-men-earned-more-than-their-white-black-and-hispanic-counterparts-in-2017.htm

12   Monnica Williams, "Colorblind Ideology Is a Form of Racism," *Psychology Today*, December 2011, https://www.psychologytoday.com/us/blog/culturally-speaking/201112/colorblind-ideology-is-form-racism

13   Eduardo Bonilla-Silva, *Racism without Racists: Color-Blind Racism and the Persistence of Racial Inequality in America*. Washington, DC: Rowman & Littlefield, 2009.

14   James Lindsay, "Racism (Systemic)," *New Discourses*, 2020, https://new-discourses.com/tftw-racism-systemic/

15   Carlos Hoyt Jr., "The Pedagogy of the Meaning of Racism: Reconciling a Discordant Discourse," *Social Work 57*, 2012, 3: pp. 225–234.

16   Jonathan Greenblatt, "Louis Farrakhan's Pleas for Justice Are Blunted by Bigotry and Calls to Violence," *Washington Post*, October 8, 2015, https://www.washingtonpost.com/opinions/louis-farrakhans-pleas-for-justice-are-blunted-by-bigotry-and-calls-to-violence/2015/10/08/3518ddca-6dd3-11e5-aa5b-f78a98956699_story.html

17   Dustin Dwyer, "Why All White People Are Racist, but Can't Handle Being Called Racist: The Theory of White Fragility," *State of Opportunity*, 2015, https://stateofopportunity.michiganradio.org/post/why-all-white-people-are-racist-cant-handle-being-called-racist-theory-white-fragility

18   James Lindsay, "White Fragility," *New Discourses*, 2020, https://newdiscourses.com/tftw-white-fragility/

19   Lindsay, "White Women's Tears (White Girl Tears)," *New Discourses*, 2020, https://newdiscourses.com/tftw-white-womens-tears/

20   Lindsay, "White Ignorance," *New Discourses*, 2020, https://newdiscourses.com/tftw-white-ignorance/

21   Lindsay, "White Complicity," *New Discourses*, 2020, https://newdiscourses.com/tftw-white-complicity/

22   Derrick A. Bell, "Brown v. Board of Education and the Interest Convergence Dilemma," *Harvard Law Review*, 93, 1980, pp. 518–533. https://harvardlawreview.org/wp-content/uploads/1980/01/518-533_Online.pdf

23   Bari Weiss, "The Miseducation of America's Elites," *City Journal*, https://www.city-journal.org/the-miseducation-of-americas-elites

24   Christopher F. Rufo, "Merchants of Revolution," *City Journal*, 2021, https://www.city-journal.org/california-ethnic-studies-programs-merchants-of-revolution

25   https://christopherrufo.com/articles/

26   "Critical Race Training in Education: K-12," https://criticalrace.org/k-12/

27   Brandon Showalter, "Scholars Warn of Dangers of Critical Race Theory, How It's Being Injected into Students," *Christian Post*, 2021, https://www.christianpost.com/us/scholars-warn-of-dangers-of-critical-race-theory.html

28   Libby Emmons, "HYPOCRISY: Left-Wing Media Suddenly Cares about Riots and Attacks on Federal Buildings After Covering for Antifa All Year," *Post Millennial*, 2021, https://thepostmillennial.com/hypocrisy-the-media-celebrated-violent-riots-for-left-wing-causes/

29   "Critical Race Training in Education: Schools," https://criticalrace.org/schools

30   Lia Eustachewich, "Coca-Cola Slammed for Diversity Training that Urged Workers to Be 'Less White,'" *New York Post*, February 23, 2021, https://nypost.com/2021/02/23/coca-cola-diversity-training-urged-workers-to-be-less-white/

31   Marcus Burke, "How the Media and Entertainment Industry Is Addressing Systemic Racism," World Economic Forum, July 2020, https://www.weforum.org/agenda/2020/07/how-media-and-entertainment-advertising-consumer-products-sports-industry-is-addressing-systemic-racism/

32   Justin Simien, Yvette Bowser, Stephanie Allain, and Julia Lebedev (Executive Producers). *Dear White People* [TV Series], Netflix, https://www.netflix.com/title/80095698?source=35

33   Cartoon Network, *See Color | The Crystal Gems Say Be Anti-Racist* [Video], YouTube, 2021, https://www.youtube.com/watch?v=zJkVgGYm4xo

34   "Racial Justice," *Sesame Street in Communities,* sesamestreetincommunities.org/topics/racial-justice/

35   Cydney Henderson, "'Kids, Race and Unity': Alicia Keys Hosts Star-Studded Nickelodeon Racism Special for Kids," *USA Today*, June 29, 2020, www.usatoday.com/story/entertainment/tv/2020/06/29/alicia-keys-hosts-star-studded-nickelodeon-racism-special-kids/3281583001/

36   Tom Kertscher, "Fact-Checking Claim about Deaths, Damage from Black Lives Matter Protests," *Austin American-Statesman*, August 10, 2020, https://www.statesman.com/story/news/politics/elections/2020/08/10/fact-checking-claim-about-deaths-damage-from-black-lives-matter-protests/113878088/

37   Jennifer Kingson, "Exclusive: $1 billion-Plus Riot Damage Is Most Expensive in Insurance History," *Axios*, 2020, https://www.axios.com/riots-cost-property-damage-276c9bcc-a455-4067-b06a-66f9db4cea9c.html

38   Steve Guest [@SteveGuest], "CNN's Chris Cuomo: 'Please, Show Me Where It Says Protesters Are Supposed to Be Polite and Peaceful,'" June 2, 2020. [Tweet]. Twitter. https://twitter.com/SteveGuest/status/1267987525198585856?

39   Nellie Andreeva and Dominic Patten, "Media Companies Voice Support for Black Lives Matter Amid Massive Protests over George Floyd Death—Update," *Deadline*, May 2020, https://deadline.com/2020/05/netflix-tweets-support-black-lives-matter-protests-george-floyd-death-1202947463/

40   Ashley Rae Goldenberg, "279 Companies Supporting Violent Antifa & Black Lives Matter," *Reality Check*, June 9, 2020, https://realityandde-

nial.wordpress.com/2020/06/09/279-companies-supporting-violent-an-
tifa-black-lives-matter/

41   Sonia Rao, "Celebrities Are Rushing to Support the Black Lives Matter
     Movement. Some Might Actually Make an Impact," *Washington Post*,
     June 11, 2020, https://www.washingtonpost.com/arts-
     entertainment/2020/06/11/celebrities-black-lives-matter-movement/

42   Benny Johnson [@bennyjohnson], "This Is the Democrat Nominee for
     VP Instigating Violent Riots that Have Left Multiple Americans Dead,"
     August 30, 2020, [Tweet], Twitter,
     https://twitter.com/bennyjohnson/status/1300197070276620288

43   Emily Czachor, "Chinese Official Condemns 'Systemic' Racism in U.S.,
     Hate Crimes Against Asian Americans," *Newsweek*, 2021,
     https://www.newsweek.com/chinese-official-condemns-systemic-rac-
     ism-us-hate-crimes-against-asian-americans-1581453

44   "Systemic Racism in US," *Iran Press*, https://iranpress.com/tag/11679-
     systemic-racism-in-us

45   Vijeta Uniyal, "China Weaponizes Social Justice Warriors and Black
     Lives Matter In Covert War Against the U.S.," *Legal Insurrection*, March
     2021, https://legalinsurrection.com/2021/03/china-weaponizes-social-
     justice-warriors-and-black-lives-matter-in-covert-war-against-the-u-s/

46   Michael W. Chapman, "Biden After Verdict: 'Systemic Racism' Is 'a Stain
     on Our Nation's Soul,'" CNS News, 2021, https://www.cnsnews.com/ar-
     ticle/washington/michael-w-chapman/biden-after-verdict-systemic-rac-
     ism-stain-our-nations-soul; Ryan Struyk, "Kamala Harris: 'We Do Have
     Two Systems of Justice in America,'" CNN, September 6, 2020,
     https://www.cnn.com/2020/09/06/politics/kamala-harris-two-justice-
     systems-cnntv/index.html; Brittany Berstein, "Biden's U.N. Ambassador:
     'White Supremacy Is Weaved into Our Founding Documents and Princi-
     ples,'" *National Review*, 2021, https://www.msn.com/en-
     us/news/world/biden-s-u-n-ambassador-white-supremacy-is-weaved-int
     o-our-founding-documents-and-principles/ar-
     BB1fEKUU?ocid=uxbndlbing

47   Marina Watts, "In Smithsonian Race Guidelines, Rational Thinking and
     Hard Work Are White Values," *Newsweek*, 2020,
     https://www.newsweek.com/smithsonian-race-guidelines-rational-
     thinking-hard-work-are-white-values-1518333

48   Ben McDonald, "Seattle Public Schools Say Math Is Racist," *Daily Caller*,
     October 21, 2019, https://dailycaller.com/2019/10/21/seattle-schools-
     math-is-racist/

49   Ben Zeisloft, "Math Education Prof: 2+2 = 4 'Trope' Reeks of White Su-

premacy Patriarchy," *Campus Reform*, 2020, https://www.campusreform.org/?ID=15409

50   Brendan Byrne, "Math Is Racist and Suffers from White Supremacy, According to Bill Gates-Funded Course," *Insider Paper*, 2020, https://insiderpaper.com/math-is-racist-white-supremacy-bill-gates/

51   "Teachers Forced to Analyze 'White Supremacy Characteristics' in the Classroom," n.d. *What Are They Learning?* https://whataretheylearning.com/detail/258/

52   Jonathan Turley, "'We Cannot Mince Words': San Francisco Education Official Denounces Meritocracy as Racist," 2021, https://jonathanturley.org/2021/02/07/we-cannot-mince-words-san-francisco-education-official-denounces-meritocracy-as-racist/

53   James Lindsay, "Ways of Knowing," *New Discourses,* 2020, https://newdiscourses.com/tftw-ways-of-knowing/

54   Lindsay, "Master's Tools," *New Discourses*, 2020, https://newdiscourses.com/tftw-masters-tools/

55   Christopher Rufo, "Critical Race Theory Would Not Solve Racial Inequality: It Would Deepen It," The Heritage Foundation, 2021, https://www.heritage.org/progressivism/report/critical-race-theory-would-not-solve-racial-inequality-it-would-deepen-it

56   Rudyard Kipling, "The White Man's Burden," 1899, https://www.bartleby.com/364/169.html

57   Savala Trepczynski, "People of Color Learn at a Young Age That They Must Be Twice as Good. Now White People Need to Be Twice as Kind," *Time*, 2020, https://time.com/5871387/white-people-must-be-twice-as-kind/

58   Tristan Fitz, "The Contradictions of Critical Theory and Counseling," *New Discourses*, July 2020, https://newdiscourses.com/2020/07/contradictions-critical-theory-counseling/

59   Lukianoff and Haidt. *The Coddling of the American Mind: How Good Intentions and Bad Ideas are Setting Up a Generation for Failure.* New York: Penguin Books.

CHAPTER 3

1   "Cultural Marxism," n.d. *Conservapedia*, https://conservapedia.com/Cultural_Marxism

2   "Antonio Gramsci." n.d. Marxists.org. https://www.marxists.org/archive/gramsci/index.htm

3   "Long March through the Institutions," n.d. *Conservapedia*, https://www.conservapedia.com/Long_march_through_the_institutions

4   "Lecture by Yuri Bezmenov," Bezmenov.net, 2020, https://bezmenov.net/lecture/

5   Frank Bruni, "Republicans Have Found Their Cruel New Culture War," *New York Times*, April 10, 2021, https://www.nytimes.com/2021/04/10/opinion/sunday/transgender-rights-republicans-arkansas.html

6   Dream McClinton, "Cardi B and Megan Thee Stallion's WAP Should Be Celebrated, Not Scolded," *The Guardian*, August 12, 2020, https://www.theguardian.com/music/2020/aug/12/cardi-b-megan-thee-stallion-wap-celebrated-not-scolded

7   Stephanie Wang, "Same-Sex Marriage: Why People Really Oppose It," *USA Today*, March 2, 2015, https://www.usatoday.com/story/news/nation/2015/03/02/same-sex-marriage-why-people-really-oppose-it/24296403/

8   Rosemarie Ho, "Want to Dismantle Capitalism? Abolish the Family," *The Nation*, s019, https://www.thenation.com/article/archive/want-to-dismantle-capitalism-abolish-the-family/

9   David Williams, "Protesters Tore Down a George Washington Statue and Set a Fire on Its Head," CNN, June 19, 2020, https://www.cnn.com/2020/06/19/us/portland-george-washington-statue-toppled-trnd/index.html

10   Lawrence R. Samuel, "Is the American Flag a Symbol of Racism?" *Psychology Today*, 2020, https://www.psychologytoday.com/us/blog/psychology-yesterday/202007/is-the-american-flag-symbol-racism

11   James Lindsay, "Cultural Marxism," *New Discourses*, 2020, https://newdiscourses.com/tftw-cultural-marxism/

12   Karl Marx: "Letter to Nikolai Danielson," St. Petersburg, Russia. February 19, 1881. International Publishers (1968), Marxist.org, https://www.marxists.org/archive/marx/works/1881/letters/81_02_19.htm

13   James Lindsay, "Critical Theory," *New Discourses*, 2020, https://newdiscourses.com/tftw-critical-theory/

14   Complaints made by students, traditional academics, and outside observers regarding the activist (vs scholarly) character of the various "critical" fields (e.g., the "studies" fields) are thus well-founded.

15   "Eros and Civilization," n.d. Marcuse.org., https://www.marcuse.org/herbert/publications/1950s/1955-eros-and-civilization.html

16   Herbert Marcuse, "An Essay on Liberation," 1969, https://www.marx-ists.org/reference/archive/marcuse/works/1969/essay-liberation.htm

17   Other important influences include the black nationalist, Black Power, and women's liberation movements. See, David Azerrad, "The Promises and Perils of Identity Politics," The Heritage Foundation, January 23, 2019, https://www.heritage.org/progressivism/report/the-promises-and-perils-identity-politics

18   Robert Paul Wolff, Barrington Moore, and Herbert Marcuse, *A Critique of Pure Tolerance*. Boston: Beacon Press, 1969, pp. 95–137. https://www.marcuse.org/herbert/publications/1960s/1965-repressive-tolerance-fulltext.html

19   Postmodernism (definition), https://www.merriam-webster.com/diction-ary/postmodern

20   Helen Pluckrose, "How French 'Intellectuals' Ruined the West: Postmod-ernism & Its Impact," *New Discourses*, 2020, https://newdiscourses.com/2020/04/french-intellectuals-ruined-west-postmodernism-impact/

21   Ideacity, Jordan Peterson | *Political Correctness and Postmodernism* [Video], 2017, YouTube, https://www.youtube.com/watch?v=f5rU-PatnXSE

22   David Satter, "100 Years of Communism—and 100 Million Dead," *Wall Street Journal*, 2017, https://www.wsj.com/articles/100-years-of-com-munismand-100-million-dead-1510011810

23   Michel Foucault, *The Order of Things*. New York: Pantheon Books, 1970.

24   Jacques Derrida, "Signature, Event, Context," *Limited Inc*. Evanston, IL: Northwestern University Press, 1988.

25   Derrida, *Positions*. Chicago: University of Chicago Press, 1981.

26   David Harsanyi, "'Words Are Violence' Is the Slogan of Tyranny," *New York Post*, June 21, 2020, https://nypost.com/2020/06/21/words-are-vio-lence-is-the-slogan-of-tyranny/

27   Steerpike. "Science Must Fall: It's Time to Decolonize Science," *The Spec-tator*, 2016, https://www.spectator.co.uk/article/science-must-fall-it-s-time-to-decolonise-science

28   Christophe de Ray, "How to (Really) Decolonise the Curriculum," *Notes to the Underground Church*, April 2021, https://notestotheunderground-church.blogspot.com/2021/04/how-to-really-decolonise-curriculum.html

29   Diane Ravitch, "Ethnomathematics," Hoover Institution, 2005, https://www.hoover.org/research/ethnomathematics

30   Helen Pluckrose and James Lindsay, *Cynical Theories: How Activist Scholarship Made Everything about Race, Gender, and Identity—and Why This Harms Everybody*. Durham, NC: Pitchstone Publishing.

31   Kimberlé Crenshaw, "Mapping the Margins: Intersectionality, Identity Politics, and Violence against Women of Color," *Stanford Law Review*, 43(6), 1991, pp. 1241–1299.

32   Crenshaw, "Mapping the Margins."

33   "Critical Legal Studies Movement," n.d. *The Bridge*, https://cyber.harvard.edu/bridge/CriticalTheory/critical2.htm

34   "Critical Legal Theory," n.d. Legal Information Institute, https://www.law.cornell.edu/wex/critical_legal_theory

35   Duncan Kennedy, "The Critique of Rights in Critical Legal Studies," In Wendy Brown and Janet Halley (Eds.), *Left Legalism/Left Critique*. Durham, NC: Duke University Press, 2002, pp. 179–227.

36   James Lindsay, "Social Constructivism," *New Discourses*, 2020, https://newdiscourses.com/tftw-social-constructivism/

37   Peggy McIntosh, "White Privilege: Unpacking the Invisible Knapsack," *Peace and Freedom*, 1989, https://psychology.umbc.edu/files/2016/10/White-Privilege_McIntosh-1989.pdf

38   Robin DiAngelo, *White Fragility: Why It's So Hard for White People to Talk About Racism*. Boston: Beacon Press.

39   Richard Delgado, "Storytelling for Oppositionists and Others: A Plea for Narrative," *Michigan Law Review*, 1989, 87(8), pp. 2411–2441, https://doi.org/10.2307/1289308; "First Amendment Formalism is Giving Way to First Amendment Legal Realism," *Harvard Civil Rights-Civil Liberties Law Review* 29, 1994, 169. https://scholarship.law.ua.edu/fac_articles/459/

40   Derrick Bell, "Serving Two Masters: Integration Ideals and Client Interests in School Desegregation Litigation," *Yale Law Journal*, 85(4), 1976, pp. 470–516, https://digitalcommons.law.yale.edu/ylj/vol85/iss4/2/

41   Marina Watts, "In Smithsonian Race Guidelines, Rational Thinking and Hard Work Are White Values, "*Newsweek*, 2020, https://www.newsweek.com/smithsonian-race-guidelines-rational-thinking-hard-work-are-white-values-1518333

42   Jeffrey J. Pyle, "Race, Equality, and the Rule of Law: Critical Race Theory's Attack on the Promises of Liberalism," *Boston College Law Review*, 40(3), pp. 787–827, http://lawdigitalcommons.bc.edu/bclr/vol40/iss3/6

CHAPTER 4

1   Dewey Cornell and Susan P. Limber, "Law and Policy on the Concept of Bullying at School," *American Psychologist*, 70(4), 2015, pp. 333–343. https://doi.org/10.1037/a0038558

2   Ann Monroe, "Shame Solutions: How Shame Impacts School-Aged Children and What Teachers Can Do to Help," *Educational Forum*, 73:1, pp. 58–66, DOI, 2008: 10.1080/00131720802539614; Patrizia Velotti, Carlo Garofalo, Federica Bottazzi, and Vincenzo Caretti, "Faces of Shame: Implications for Self-Esteem, Emotion Regulation, Aggression, and Well-Being," *Journal of Psychology*, 151:2, 171 Vincenzo 184, DOI, 2017: 10.1080/00223980.2016.1248809

3   Yan Zhang, Lening Zhang, and Francis Benton, "Hate Crimes Against Asian Americans," *American Journal of Criminal Justice*, 2021, https://doi.org/10.1007/s12103-020-09602-9

4   John Murawski, "Critical Race Theory Is About to Face Its Day(s) in Court," *RealClearInvestigations*, 2021, https://www.realclearinvestigations.com/articles/2021/04/27/critical_race_theory_is_about_to_face_its_days_in_court_774290.html

5   House Un-American Activities Committee. n.d. Harry S. Truman Library. https://www.trumanlibrary.gov/education/presidential-inquiries/house-un-american-activities-committee

6   Morgan Phillips, "Biden Calls Recent Spike in Anti-Semitic Attacks 'Despicable, Unconscionable, un-American,'" Fox News, 2021, https://www.msn.com/en-us/news/politics/biden-calls-recent-spike-in-anti-semitic-attacks-e2-80-98despicable-unconscionable-un-american-e2-80-99/ar-AAKuSRQ

7   Chris Sommerfeldt, "'We're All Hurt by this Hate': Biden Signs Bill to Crack Down on Anti-Asian Attacks," *Daily News*, 2021, https://www.msn.com/en-us/news/politics/e2-80-98we-e2-80-99re-all-hurt-by-this-hate-e2-80-99-biden-signs-bill-to-crack-down-on-anti-asian-attacks/ar-AAKcZiM

8   The memorandum was technically written on behalf of the president by OMB Director Russell Vought. See: https://www.whitehouse.gov/wp-content/uploads/2020/09/M-20-34.pdf

9   Robert Longley, "What Is Classical Liberalism? Definition and Examples," *ThoughtCo.*, 2020, https://www.thoughtco.com/classical-liberalism-definition-4774941

10 Richard Delgado and Jean Stefancic, *Critical Race Theory: An Introduction* (2nd Edition). New York: NYU Press, 2012.

11   Delgado and Stefancic, *Must We Defend Nazis? Why the First Amendment Should Not Protect Hate Speech and White Supremacy*. New York: NYU Press, 1997.

12   Roberto Unger, "The Critical Legal Studies Movement," *Harvard Law Review*, 96(3), pp. 561–675, 1983, https://doi.org/10.2307/1341032

13   Duncan Kennedy, "Form and Substance in Private Law Adjudication," *Harvard Law Review*, 89, 1976, pp. 1685–1778, https://duncankennedy.net/documents/Form%20and%20Substance%20in%20Private%20Law%20Adjudication.pdf

14   Daria Roithmayr, "Deconstructing the Distinction Between Bias and Merit," *California Law Review*, 85(5), 1998, pp. 1449–1507. https://doi.org/10.2307/3481064

15   Jeffrey J. Pyle, "Race, Equality, and the Rule of Law: Critical Race Theory's Attack on the Promises of Liberalism," *Boston College Law Review*, 40, 1999, pp. 787–827. https://lawdigitalcommons.bc.edu/bclr/vol40/iss3/6

16   Paul Butler, "Racially Based Jury Nullification: Black Power in the Criminal Justice System," *Yale Law Journal*, 105, 1995, pp. 677–725, https://digitalcommons.law.yale.edu/ylj/vol105/iss3/5/

17   Derrick Bell, "Racial Realism," *Connecticut Law Review*, 24(2), 1992, pp. 363–379.

18   Cheryl L. Harris, "Whiteness as Property," *Harvard Law Review*, 1993, https://harvardlawreview.org/1993/06/whiteness-as-property/

19   Ibram X. Kendi, n.d. "Pass an Anti-Racist Constitutional Amendment," *Politico*, 2019, https://www.politico.com/interactives/2019/how-to-fix-politics-in-america/inequality/pass-an-anti-racist-constitutional-amendment/

20   Carol M. Swain, *The New White Nationalism in America: Its Challenge to Integration*. Cambridge: Cambridge University Press, 2002.

21   Hans Kohn, *The Idea of Nationalism: A Study in Its Origins and Background*. New York: MacMillan Publishers, 1944.

22   National Geographic Society, "Gettysburg Address, "*National Geographic*, 2020, https://www.nationalgeographic.org/encyclopedia/gettysburg-address/

23   Gunnar Myrdal, "An American Dilemma," in Michael W. Hughey (ed.) *New Tribalisms: Main Trends of the Modern World*. New York: Palgrave Macmillan, 1962, https://doi.org/10.1007/978-1-349-26403-2_5

24   Abraham Lincoln, "Letter to Henry L. Pierce and Others," in Roy P. Basler (ed.) *Collected Works of Abraham Lincoln*, 1859. Ann Arbor, MI:

University of Michigan Digital Library Production Services

25 Timothy Sandefur, "Frederick Douglass's 'Glorious Liberty Document,'" *In Defense of Liberty*, 2020, https://indefenseofliberty.blog/2020/02/13/frederick-douglasss-glorious-liberty-document/

26 Frederick Douglass, "What to the Slave is the Fourth of July?" 2020, https://www.owleyes.org/text/what-to-the-slave-is-the-fourth-of-july/read/text-of-douglasss-speech

27 Defenders of Ssavery likewise understood that the nation's founding values were incompatible with slavery. In his *Disquisition on Government* (1851), John C. Calhoun attacks the Declaration of Independence on these grounds.

28 Martin Luther King Jr., "The American Dream," 1965, https://singju-post.com/the-american-dream-martin-luther-king-jr-full-transcript/

29 Larry Arnn, Carol M. Swain, and Matthew Spalding, *The 1776 Report*, 2021, https://f.hubspotusercontent10.net/hubfs/397762/The%20President%E2%80%99s%20Advisory%201776%20Commission%20-%20Final%20Report.pdf

30 *1619 Project*, https://www.nytimes.com/interactive/2019/08/14/magazine/1619-america-slavery.html

31 Liv Finne, "The 1619 Project: Sloppy Scholarship and Distorted History Under Consideration for Washington Schools," Washington Policy Center, 2020, https://www.washingtonpolicy.org/library/doclib/Finne-The-1619-Project-Sloppy-scholarship-and-distorted-history-under-consideration-for-Washington-schools..pdf

32 Leslie M. Harris, "I Helped Fact-Check the 1619 Project. The Times Ignored Me," *Politico*, March 6, 2020, https://www.politico.com/news/magazine/2020/03/06/1619-project-new-york-times-mistake-122248

33 Ben Johnson, "The 1619 Projection: 3 Lies Pulitzer Should Not Reward," 2020, Acton Institute, https://www.acton.org/publications/transatlantic/2020/05/18/1619-projection-3-lies-pulitzer-should-not-reward

34 Carol M. Swain, "Racial Supremacy and Covenantal Reconciliation," in Gerald McDermott (ed.) *Race and Covenant: Recovering the Religious Roots for American Reconciliation*. Grand Rapids, MI: Acton Institute.

35 Alistair Boddy-Evans, "The Role of Islam in Slavery in Africa," *ThoughtCo*, 2019, https://www.thoughtco.com/the-role-of-islam-in-african-slavery-44532

36 Zach Goldberg, "How the Media Led the Great Racial Awakening,"

Tablet, 2020, https://www.tabletmag.com/sections/news/articles/media-great-racial-awakening

37   Eric Kaufmann, "The Media Is Creating a False Perception of Rising Racism. My New Study Proves It," *Newsweek*, 2021, https://www.newsweek.com/media-creating-false-perception-rising-racism-my-new-study-proves-it-opinion-1583264

38   Christopher Schorr, "Research Shows Critical Race Theory Is Actually Making People More Racist," *The Federalist*, 2020, https://thefederalist.com/2020/10/19/research-shows-critical-race-theory-is-actually-making-people-more-racist/

39   Carol M. Swain, *The New White Nationalism in America: its Challenge to Integration*. Cambridge: Cambridge University Press, 2002.

40   Blood libel (definition), https://www.merriam-webster.com/dictionary/blood%20libel

CHAPTER 5

1   Lawrence Meyers, "Politics Really Is Downstream from Culture," *Breitbart*, August 22, 2011, https://www.breitbart.com/entertainment/2011/08/22/politics-really-is-downstream-from-culture/

2   "Colleges and Universities with Religious Affiliations," n.d. Encyclopedia.com, https://www.encyclopedia.com/education/encyclopedias-almanacs-transcripts-and-maps/colleges-and-universities-religious-affiliations

3   Carol M. Swain, *Be The People: A Call to Reclaim America's Faith and Promise*. Nashville: Thomas Nelson Publishers, 2011.

4   Daniel Elazar, *The Covenant Tradition in Politics*. Piscataway, NJ: Transaction Publishers, 1995.

5   Robert Bellah, "Civil Religion in America," *Dædalus*, 96(1), 1967, pp. 1–21. http://www.robertbellah.com/articles_5.htm

6   Mark David Hall, "Did America Have a Christian Founding?" The Heritage Foundation, 2011, https://www.heritage.org/political-process/report/did-america-have-christian-founding

7   Lyndon B. Johnson, "Special Message to Congress: The American Promise," *Public Papers of the Presidents of the United States: Lyndon B. Johnson*, 1965 (Vol. 1). Washington, DC: Government Printing Office, http://web.mit.edu/21h.102/www/Primary%20source%20collections/Civil%20Rights/We_Shall_Overcome.htm

8   "Preserving a Constitution Designed for a Moral and Religious People," Regent University, 2020, https://ccta.regent.edu/2020/08/03/preserving-a-constitution-designed-for-a-moral-and-religious-people/

9   "Thomas Jefferson to Thomas Law," n.d. *Founders Online,* June 13, 1814.https://founders.archives.gov/documents/Jefferson/03-07-02-0307

10   "Farewell Address," n.d. *Founders Online,* September 19, 1796, https://founders.archives.gov/documents/Washington/05-20-02-0440-0002

11   "From John Adams to Massachusetts Militia," n.d. *Founders Online,* October 11, 1798, https://founders.archives.gov/documents/Adams/99-02-02-3102

12   Barry Kosmin and Seymour Lachman, *One Nation Under God: Religion in Contemporary American Society.* New York: Harmony Books, 2011.

13   Alexis de Tocqueville, *Democracy in America*, 1835, http://seas3.elte.hu/coursematerial/LojkoMiklos/Alexis-de-Tocqueville-Democracy-in-America.pdf

14   Mark Tooley, "Eisenhower's Religion," *American Spectator*, 2011, https://spectator.org/eisenhowers-religion/

15   Donald Lutz, "The Relative Influence of European Writers on Late Eighteenth Century American Political Thought," *American Political Science Review*, 78(1), 1984, pp. 189–197, https://doi.org/10.2307/1961257

16   Barry Shain, *The Myth of American Individualism*. Princeton, NJ: Princeton University Press, 1994.

17   Feross Aboukhadijeh, "Scientific and Religious Transformation," Study-Notes.org, 2012, https://www.apstudynotes.org/us-history/topics/scientific-and-religious-transformation/

18   Dominic Erdozain, "Faith Against Faith: Recovering the Religious Character of the Enlightenment," *ABC Religion and Ethics,* 2019, https://www.abc.net.au/religion/recovering-the-religious-character-of-the-enlightenment/11278006

19   Constitutional Rights Foundation, "St. Thomas Aquinas, Natural Law, and the Common Good," *Bill of Rights in Action,* 22(4), 2006, https://www.crf-usa.org/bill-of-rights-in-action/bria-22-4-c-st-thomas-aquinas-natural-law-and-the-common-good

20   This isn't to say that there aren't strong Christian arguments against rebellion (e.g., Romans 13).

21   Aquinas drew heavily on classical thinkers (especially Aristotle) but also on the Bible (Romans 2:14–15). However one attributes the parentage of natural law, it shaped the Christian worldview.

22 It should be added that Christianity's role in shaping Western morality was even more profound. See *Dominion* (2019) by Tom Holland and "Christianity and the Roots of Human Dignity in Late Antiquity" by Kyle Harper in Shah and Hertzke's *Christianity and Freedom*.

23 Ofir Haivry and Yoram Hazony, "What Is Conservatism?" *American Affairs*, 1(2), 2017, https://americanaffairsjournal.org/2017/05/what-is-conservatism/

24 Yoram Hazony, *The Virtue of Nationalism*. New York: Basic Books, 2018.

25 Rod Dreher, "Antiracist, Anti-Christian," *American Conservative*, 2021, https://www.theamericanconservative.com/dreher/kendi-antiracist-anti-christian-critical-race-theory/

26 Woke Preacher Clips, Ibram Kendi: *Antiracists Fundamentally Reject "Savior Theology" and Embrace Liberation Theology* [Video], YouTube, 2021, https://www.youtube.com/watch?v=azJh4N69Q5k&t=161s

27 Neil Shenvi, n.d. "Conflicts Between Critical Theory and Christianity," *Shenvi Apologetics,* https://shenviapologetics.com/social-justice-critical-theory-and-christianity-are-they-compatible-part-3-2/

28 Williamson M. Evers, "California Leftists Try to Cancel Math Class," 2021, *Wall Street Journal*, https://www.wsj.com/articles/california-left-ists-try-to-cancel-math-class-11621355858?st=wkwyuldduncjej7

29 James Lindsay, "Ways of Knowing," *New Discourses,* 2020, https://new-discourses.com/tftw-ways-of-knowing/

30 Neil Shenvi, n.d. "Conflicts Between CT and Christianity," *Shenvi Apologetics,* https://shenviapologetics.com/christianity-and-critical-theory-part-2/

31 Derrick Bell, "Racial Realism," *Connecticut Law Review*, 24(2), 1992, pp. 363–379. http://blog.richmond.edu/criticalracetheory/files/2019/02/Bell-Racial-Realism.pdf

32 Joshua Lawson, "You Can Be a Christian, You Can Be a Marxist, But You Can't Be Both," *The Federalist*, 2020, https://thefederalist.com/2020/06/11/you-can-be-christian-you-can-be-marxist-but-you-cant-be-both/

33 A metanarrative is "an overarching account or interpretation of events and circumstances that provides a pattern or structure for people's beliefs and gives meaning to their experiences." See, Metanarrative (definition), Lexico.com, https://www.lexico.com/en/definition/metanarrative

34 Wilfred Reilly, "'Systemic Racism' Is a Conspiracy Theory," *Spiked*, 2021, https://www.spiked-online.com/2021/02/10/systemic-racism-is-a-con-spiracy-theory/

35 Douglas Ernst, "Sarah Jeong's Racist Tweets Spotlighted After New York

Times Hiring: 'White Men Are Bulls—,'" *Washington Times*, August 2, 2018, https://www.washingtontimes.com/news/2018/aug/2/sarah-jeongs-racist-tweets-spotlighted-after-nytim/

36 Tristan Justice, "28 Times Media and Democrats Excused or Endorsed Violence Committed By Left-Wing Activists," *The Federalist*, January 7, 2021, https://thefederalist.com/2021/01/07/28-times-media-and-democrats-excused-or-endorsed-violence-committed-by-left-wing-activists/

37 Fuzzy Slippers, "You Will Be Made to Bow: White Leftists Kneel Before Blacks They Harmed by Being Born White," *Legal Insurrection*, June 2020, https://legalinsurrection.com/2020/06/you-will-be-made-to-bow-white-leftists-kneel-before-blacks-they-harmed-by-being-born-white/

38 Darlena Cunha, "Ferguson: In Defense of Rioting," *Time*, 2014, https://time.com/3605606/ferguson-in-defense-of-rioting/

39 Sam Harris, "Sleepwalking toward Armageddon," 2014, https://samharris.org/sleepwalking-toward-armageddon/

40 Rick Plasterer, "How the Personal Becomes the Tyrannical," *Juice Ecumenism*, October 25, 2019, https://juicyecumenism.com/2019/10/25/personal-becomes-tyrannical/

41 Christopher C. Lund, "Title VII and Religious Exemptions," *Civil Liberties in the United States*, 2012, https://uscivilliberties.org/themes/4599-title-vii-and-religious-exemptions.html

42 *School Dist. of Abington Township v. Schempp*, 374 U. S. 203 (1963).

43 "Critical Race Training in Education," https://criticalrace.org/

44 Michael Vlahos, "Church of Woke: Next American Religion?" Center for the Study of Statesmanship, 2021, https://css.cua.edu/humanitas_journal/church-of-woke/

45 John McWhorter, "Antiracism, Our Flawed New Religion," *Daily Beast*, 2017, https://www.thedailybeast.com/antiracism-our-flawed-new-religion

46 There is no agreed-upon term for the phenomenon under consideration. We think that "Critical Race Theory" speaks best to the modern manifestation of this phenomenon. Others refer to "Critical Theory" or "Cultural Marxism" to cast a wider net over Marx-influenced social theories. "Identity politics" or "grievance studies" roughly does the same.

47 Brooke Singman, "Biden, Harris Slam 'Systemic Racism' in US, Say "Chauvin Guilty Verdict Is 'Giant Step' toward Racial Justice," Fox News, 2021, https://www.foxnews.com/politics/biden-harris-say-chauvin-guilty-verdict-is-giant-step-toward-racial-justice-call-for-congress-to-act

48 *Psaki Comments on Fatal Police Shooting of Teen Ma'Khia Bryant* [Video],

n.d. Daily Mail, https://www.dailymail.co.uk/video/news/video-2403394/Video-Psaki-comments-fatal-police-shooting-teen-MaKhia-Bryant.html

49   Ed Dingess, "Jemar Tisby Denies the Gospel, Insists White People Must Atone for Their Own Past Sins," *Reformation Charlotte*, February 13, 2019, https://reformationcharlotte.org/2019/02/13/jemar-tisby-denies-the-gospel-insists-white-people-must-atone-for-their-own-past-sins/

50   Jeff Maples, "Thabiti Anyabwile Says Opposing Reparations for Blacks Comes from the Devil," *Reformation Charlotte*, March 16, 2019, https://reformationcharlotte.org/2019/03/16/thabiti-anyabwile-says-opposing-reparations-for-blacks-comes-from-the-devil/

51   F. A. Grabowski, "The Church of Woke: A Parody of Faith," *Crisis Magazine*, 2020, https://www.crisismagazine.com/2020/the-church-of-woke-a-parody-of-faith

52   Sean Collins, "Wokeness: Old Religion in a New Bottle," *Spiked*, August 14, 2020, https://www.spiked-online.com/2020/08/14/wokeness-old-religion-in-new-bottle/

53   Carol M. Swain, *Countercultural Living: What Jesus Has to Say About Life, Marriage, Race, Gender Identity, and Materialism*, unpublished manuscript, chapter 3, p. 30 (Forthcoming, September 2021).

CHAPTER 6

1   Jonathan Butcher and Mike Gonzalez., *Critical Race Theory, the New Intolerance, and Its Grip on America*, The Heritage Foundation, 2020, pp. 9–11, https://www.heritage.org/civil-rights/report/critical-race-theory-the-new-intolerance-and-its-grip-america

2   Derrick Bell, "Who's Afraid of Critical Race Theory?" *University of Illinois Law Review*, 1995, pp. 893–910.

3   Chris Demaske, "Critical Race Theory," *First Amendment Encyclopedia*, 2009, https://mtsu.edu/first-amendment/article/1254/critical-race-theory

4   See Delgado and Stefancic, 2017, p. 3; Cheryl Harris, "Whiteness as Property," *Harvard Law Review*, 1993, https://harvardlawreview.org/1993/06/whiteness-as-property/

5   Charles Lawrence, "The Word and the River: Pedagogy as Scholarship as Struggle," *Southern California Law Review*, 65, 1992, pp. 2231–2298.

6   As discussed by Butcher and Gonzalez (2020), pp. 19–23, The Obama Administration applied CRT's equity-contra-equality viewpoint ("disparate impact theory") to the nation's schools, requiring them to reduce

racial disparities in discipline. According to an appeals court ruling in *People Who Care v. Rockford Board of Education* (1997), such approaches entail "either systematically over-punishing the innocent or systematically under-punishing the guilty. They place race at war with justice."

7   Ibram X. Kendi, n.d. "Pass an Anti-Racist Constitutional Amendment," *Politico Magazine*, https://www.politico.com/interactives/2019/how-to-fix-politics-in-america/inequality/pass-an-anti-racist-constitutional-amendment/

8   Angela Harris (1994) argues that CRT inherits from traditional civil rights scholarship a "vision of liberation from racism through right reason," but that this vision is in conflict with its deconstructive roots in Critical Legal Studies. Angela Harris, "The Jurisprudence of Reconstruction," *California Law Review* 82, 4: 1994, pp. 741–785.

9   Derrick Bell, "Racial Realism," *Connecticut Law Review*, 24(2), 1992, pp. 363–379, http://blog.richmond.edu/criticalracetheory/files/2019/02/Bell-Racial-Realism.pdf

10   In "Racial Realism" (1992), Bell argues the civil rights movement's emphasis on equality under law was in error because the Constitution grants such equality to blacks.

11   Kimberlé Crenshaw, Neil Gotanda, Gary Peller, and Kendall Thomas, *Critical Race Theory: The Key Writings that Formed the Movement*. New York: The New Press, 1995, p. xvii.

12   William Tate, "Critical Race Theory and Education: History, Theory, and Implications," *Review of Research in Education 22*: 1997, pp. 195–247.

13   Paul Sperry, "Elite K-8 School Teaches White Students They're Born Racist," *New York Post*, July 1, 2016, https://nypost.com/2016/07/01/elite-k-8-school-teaches-white-students-theyre-born-racist/

14   Christopher F. Rufo, "The Wokest Place on Earth," 2021, https://christopherrufo.com/the-wokest-place-on-earth/; "Nuclear Consequences," 2020, https://christopherrufo.com/nuclear-consequences/

15   Adrienne van der Valk and Anya Malley, "What's My Complicity? Talking White Fragility with Robin DiAngelo," *Learning for Justice*, Summer 2019, https://www.learningforjustice.org/magazine/summer-2019/whats-my-complicity-talking-white-fragility-with-robin-diangelo

16   Christopher F. Rufo, "Failure Factory," 2021, https://christopherrufo.com/failure-factory/

17   Jesse Singal, "A Professor Pushed Back Against 'White Fragility' Training. The College Investigated Her for 9 Months," *Reason*, April 5, 2021, https://reason.com/2021/04/05/a-professor-pushed-back-against-white-

fragility-training-the-college-investigated-her-for-9-months/

18   Office of the Assistant Secretary for Administration & Management, n.d. "Legal Highlight: The Civil Rights Act of 1964," U.S. Department of Labor, https://www.dol.gov/agencies/oasam/civil-rights-center/statutes/civil-rights-act-of-1964

19   Office for Civil Rights, "Civil Rights Requirements - A. Title VI of the Civil Rights Act of 1964, 42 U.S.C. 2000d et seq. ('Title VI')," U.S. Department of Health & Human Services, 2013, https://www.hhs.gov/civil-rights/for-individuals/special-topics/needy-families/civil-rights-requirements/index.html

20   Office for Civil Rights, "Title IX of the Education Amendments of 1972," U.S. Department of Health & Human Services, 2020, https://www.hhs.gov/civil-rights/for-individuals/sex-discrimination/title-ix-education-amendments/index.html

21   Sam Dorman, "Legal Coalition Forming to Stop Critical Race Theory Training around the Country," Fox News, 2021, https://www.foxnews.com/politics/legal-coalition-critical-race-theory

22   John Muraswki, "Critical Race Theory About to See Its Day in Court," *Daily Signal*, April 30, 2021, https://www.dailysignal.com/2021/04/30/critical-race-theory-about-to-see-its-day-in-court/

23   Virginia Allen, "Legal Coalition to Sue to Stop Feds' Critical Race Theory Training," *Daily Signal*, February 1, 2021, https://www.dailysignal.com/2021/02/01/legal-coalition-to-sue-to-stop-feds-critical-race-theory-training/

24   The Clark Lawsuit, n.d. "No Left Turn in Education," https://noleftturn.us/the-clark-lawsuit/#1619384542554-a693ccf1-1f96

25   Susan Edelman and Selim Algar, "Fourth White DOE Executive Sues Over Racial Discrimination," *New York Post*, October 1, 2019, https://nypost.com/2019/10/01/fourth-white-doe-executive-sues-over-racial-discrimination/

26   Joseph Simonson, "Lawyer Takes on Critical Race Theory in California," *Washington Examiner*, 2021, https://www.washingtonexaminer.com/news/lawyer-takes-on-critical-race-theory-in-california

27   Michelle Goldberg, "The Campaign to Cancel Wokeness," *New York Times*, February 26, 2021, https://www.nytimes.com/2021/02/26/opinion/speech-racism-academia.html; Sachs, Jeffrey, "The New War on Woke," *ARC Digital*, 2021, https://medium.com/arc-digital/the-new-war-on-woke-ced9fd3699b

28 Gad Saad discusses the ideology of "Diversity, Inclusivity, and Equity" or "DIE." See, Gad Saad, *The Parasitic Mind: How Infectious Ideas Are Killing Common Sense.* Washington, DC: Regnery, 2020.

29 Adam Harris, "The GOP's 'Critical Race Theory' Obsession," *The Atlantic*, May 2021, https://www.theatlantic.com/politics/archive/2021/05/gops-critical-race-theory-fixation-explained/618828/?mc_cid=7e04927eac&mc_eid=da593a21b6

30 "Joe Biden Revokes Donald Trump's Order Banning 'Critical Race Theory' and Other Diversity Training Which Ex-President Called 'Un-American,'" *Daily Mail*, 2021, https://www.dailymail.co.uk/news/article-9173703/Biden-revokes-Trump-order-banning-diversity-training.html

31 Relative to the propagation of divisive concepts, HB544, 2015 Session, N.H, 2015, https://legiscan.com/NH/text/HB544/id/2238380

32 Granite State Progress, "Racial Justice Supporters Condemn White Supremacy Protection Act Hate Rally in Concord" (HB 544 & State Budget), April 24, 2021, https://granitestateprogress.org/2021/04/24/racial-justice-supporters-condemn-white-supremacy-protection-act-hate-rally-in-concord-hb-544-state-budget/

33 James Lindsay, "White Women's Tears (White Girl Tears)," *New Discourses*, 2020, https://newdiscourses.com/tftw-white-womens-tears/

34 Hans Bader, "States Should Ban Racist Falsehoods from Public School Curriculums, Such as Critical Race Theory," Liberty Unyielding, February 27, 2021, https://libertyunyielding.com/2021/02/27/states-should-ban-racist-falsehoods-from-public-school-curriculums-such-as-critical-race-theory/

35 *Student Government Association v. Board of Trustees* (1989), NAACP v. Hunt (1990), and CBS v. DNC (1973: concurring opinion).

36 *Hazelwood School District v. Kuhlmeier* (1988).

37 *Hunter v. Pittsburgh* (1907).

38 *Hayut v. State University of New York* (2003).

39 *Huckabay v. Moore* (1998); Bowen v. Missouri (2002).

40 *Creek v. Village of Westhaven* (1996).

41 *West Virginia v. Barrette* (1943)

42 Joshua Dunn, "Critical Race Theory Collides with the Law," *Education Next*, 2021, https://www.educationnext.org/critical-race-theory-collides-with-law/

43 George R. La Noue, "Critical Race Training or Civil Rights Law: We

Can't Have Both," *Law and Liberty*, 2020, https://lawliberty.org/critical-race-theory-or-civil-rights-law-we-cant-have-both/

44   Christopher F. Rufo, "Nuclear Consequences," 2020, https://christopher-rufo.com/nuclear-consequences/

45   "Baseless Accusations of Racism Are "Racial Harassment," see *Underwood v. Northport Health Services* (1989); "Employers Are Liable for Racial Harassment Claims Against Whites, see *Huckabay v. Moore* (1998); Anti-Male Diversity Training Can Be 'Harassment,'" see *Hartman v. Pena* (1995).

46   Hans Bader, "Employee Punished After Criticizing White Male Reeducation Seminar Could Sue Nuclear Weapons Lab," CNS News, 2020, https://www.cnsnews.com/commentary/hans-bader/employee-punished-after-criticizing-white-male-reeducation-seminar-could-sue

47   Sisco v. J. S. Alberici Co. (1981), Quinn v. Green Tree Credit Corporation (1998).

48   Savannah Behrmann, "Trump Says He Moved to End Racial Sensitivity Training in Federal Agencies 'Because It's Racist,'" *USA Today*, September 29, 2020, https://www.usatoday.com/story/news/politics/elections/2020/09/29/presidential-debate-trump-claims-he-moved-end-racial-sensitivity-training-federal-agencies-because-i/3583361001/

49   Kiara Alfonseca, "Critical Race Theory in the Classroom: Understanding the Debate," ABC News, 2021, https://abcnews.go.com/US/critical-race-theory-classroom-understanding-debate/story?id=77627465

50   Leah Asmelash, "A School District Tried to Address Racism, A Group of Parents Fought Back," CNN, May 5, 2021, https://www.cnn.com/2021/05/05/us/critical-race-theory-southlake-carroll-isd-trnd/index.html

51   Josh Dawsey and Jeff Stein, "White House Directs Federal Agencies to Cancel Race-Related Training Sessions It Calls 'Un-American Propaganda,'" *Washington Post*, September 4, 2020, https://www.washingtonpost.com/politics/2020/09/04/white-house-racial-sensitivity-training/

52   Christopher F. Rufo, "Critical Race Fragility," *City Journal*, 2021, https://www.city-journal.org/the-left-wont-debate-critical-race-theory

53   Christopher F. Rufo, "Woke Elementary," 2021, https://christopherrufo.com/woke-elementary/

54   Christopher F. Rufo, "Gone Crazy," *City Journal*, 2021, https://www.city-journal.org/east-side-community-school-tells-parents-to-become-white-traitors

55   Lia Eustachewich, "Coca-Cola Slammed for Diversity Training that

Urged Workers to Be 'Less White,'" *New York Post*, 2021, https://nypost.com/2021/02/23/coca-cola-diversity-training-urged-workers-to-be-less-white/

56   Kendi, *How to Be an Antiracist*, 2019, p. 19.

57   *Civil Rights Act of 1964* § 2, 42 U.S.C. § 2000e et seq (1964). https://www.ourdocuments.gov/doc.php?flash=true&doc=97&page=transcript

58   Office for Civil Rights, "Civil Rights Requirements - A. Title VI of the Civil Rights Act of 1964, 42 U.S.C. 2000d et seq. ('Title VI')," U.S. Department of Health & Human Services, 2013, https://www.hhs.gov/civil-rights/for-individuals/special-topics/needy-families/civil-rights-requirements/index.html

59   *Education Amendments Act of 1972,* 20 U.S.C. §§1681–1688 (1972).

CHAPTER 7

1   Zach Goldberg, "How the Media Led the Great Racial Awakening," *Tablet*, 2020, https://www.tabletmag.com/sections/news/articles/media-great-racial-awakening

2   Matthew Yglesias, "The Great Awokening," *Vox*, 2019, https://www.vox.com/2019/3/22/18259865/great-awokening-white-liberals-race-polling-trump-2020

3   Cass Sunstein, *Republic.com*. Princeton, NJ: Princeton University Press, 2001; *Republic.com 2.0*. Princeton, NJ: Princeton University Press, 2009.

4   Seth Flaxman, Sharad Goel, and Justin M. Rao, "Filter Bubbles, Echo Chambers, and Online News Consumption," *Public Opinion Quarterly*, 80(S1), 2016, pp. 298–320, https://doi.org/10.1093/poq/nfw006

5   David French, "Sorry Social Justice Warriors: Political Correctness Has Peaked," *National Review*, 2015, http://www.hawaiifreepress.com/Articles-Main/ID/16240/Political-Correctness-Has-Peaked vs David French, "Unhinged Activists Never Enter the 'Real World,'" *National Review*, May 28, 2017, https://www.realclearpolitics.com/2017/05/28/unhinged_activists_never_enter_the_039real_world039_411463.html

6   Joseph Ashby, "The Facts of Life Are Conservative, Even in Zuccotti Park," *American Thinker*, 2011, https://www.americanthinker.com/articles/2011/10/the_facts_of_life_are_conservative_even_in_zuccotti_park.html

7   Matthew Lohmeier, *Irresistible Revolution: Marxism's Goal of Conquest and the Unmaking of the American Military*. Self-published, 2021.

8   Oriana Pawlyk, "Space Force CO Fired over Comments about Marxism in the Military Now Subject of IG Probe," Military.com, May 20, 2021, https://www.military.com/daily-news/2021/05/20/space-force-co-fired-over-comments-about-marxism-military-now-subject-of-ig-probe.html

9   Kristina Wong, "Defense Secretary Lloyd Austin Calls for 60-Day 'Stand Down' to Discuss Extremism in the Military," *Breitbart*, February 4, 2021, https://www.breitbart.com/politics/2021/02/04/defense-secretary-lloyd-austin-calls-60-day-stand-down-discuss-extremism-military/

10   Jordan Davidson, "Democrats Rally to Purge 'Extremists' and Trump Voters from National Guard, Turning the Military into Politics," *The Federalist*, January 21, 2021, https://thefederalist.com/2021/01/21/democrats-rally-to-purge-extremists-and-trump-voters-from-national-guard-turning-the-military-into-politics/

11   "Meet Bishop Garrison: The Pentagon's Hatchet Man in Charge of Purging MAGA Patriots and Installing Race Theory in the Military," *Revolver*, May 2021, https://www.revolver.news/2021/05/bishop-garrison-pentagon-hatchet-man/

12   Frank Newport, "Public Opinion, the Role of Government, and the Candidates," *Gallup*, 2019, https://news.gallup.com/opinion/polling-matters/268799/public-opinion-role-government-candidates.aspx

13   Dakota Wood and Mike Gonzalez, "The Woke Takeover of the US Military Endangers Us All," *New York Post*, May 23, 2021, https://nypost.com/2021/05/23/the-woke-takeover-of-the-us-military-endangers-us-all/

14   Joseph Bottum, "The Spiritual Shape of Political Ideas," *The Aquila Report*, 2018, https://www.theaquilareport.com/the-spiritual-shape-of-political-ideas/; Joseph Bottum, *An Anxious Age: The Post-Protestant Ethic and the Spirit of America*. New York: Image, 2014.

15   Glenn Harlan Reynolds, "The Elite's 'Virtue Signals' Are Falling on Deaf Ears," *Times Herald*, November 7, 2017, https://www.thetimesherald.com/story/opinion/columnists/2017/11/07/elites-virtue-signals-falling-deaf-ears/107426580/

16   Tom Holland, *Dominion: How the Christian Revolution Remade the World*. London: Hachette UK, 2019.

17   Toby Young, "The Rise of the Woke Corporation," *The Spectator*, 2019, https://www.spectator.co.uk/article/the-rise-of-the-woke-corporation

18   Ashe Schow, "ESPN Hits Ratings Low, Sports Journalist Blames 'Wokecenter on Steroids' Not Coronavirus," *Daily Wire*, 2020, https://www.dailywire.com/news/espn-hits-ratings-low-sports-journalist-blames-wokecenter-on-steroids-not-coronavirus

19   Ashlianna Kreiner, "Poll: Only 28% of Americans Support HR 1—the 'For the People Act,'" CNSNews, 2021, https://www.cnsnews.com/blog/ashlianna-kreiner/poll-only-28-americans-support-hr-1-people-act

20   Gabe Kaminsky, "Delta Airlines Condemns Georgia Voter ID Law, Requires ID to Fly," *The Federalist*, 2021, https://thefederalist.com/2021/04/06/delta-airlines-condemns-georgia-voter-id-law-requires-id-to-fly/.

21   Bradford Betz, "Coca-Cola Staff Told in Online Training Seminar 'Try to Be Less White,'" Fox Business, 2021, https://www.foxbusiness.com/lifestyle/coca-cola-staff-online-training-seminar-be-less-white

22   James R. Bailey and Hillary Phillips, "How Do Consumers Feel When Companies Get Political?" *Harvard Business Review*, February 2020, https://hbr.org/2020/02/how-do-consumers-feel-when-companies-get-political

23   Zachary Warmbrodt and Victoria Guida, "Big Banks Offer 'Target-Rich Environment' for 2020 Democrats," *Politico*, April 9, 2019, https://www.politico.com/story/2019/04/09/big-banks-2020-democrats-1336018; Robby Soave, "Democratic Governors Threaten Business Owners Who Reopen Ahead of Schedule," *Politico*, May 12, 2020, https://reason.com/2020/05/12/democratic-governors-lockdown-businesses-coronavirus-covid-19/

24   Kimberly Amadeo, "Republican Views on the Economy: Republicans Economic Views and How They Work in the Real World," *The Balance*, 2021, https://www.thebalance.com/do-republican-economic-policies-work-4129139

25   Richard Hanania, "Why Is Everything Liberal?" 2021, https://richardhanania.substack.com/p/why-is-everything-liberal

26   Noah Carl, "Who Doesn't Want to Hear the Other Side's View?" 2017, https://noahcarl.medium.com/who-doesnt-want-to-hear-the-other-sides-view-9a7cdf3ad702

27   John O'Sullivan, "O'Sullivan's First Law," *National Review*, 2003, https://web.archive.org/web/20030707094659/https://www.national-review.com/flashback/flashback-jos062603.asp

28   Brad Slager, "Fox News Moves Left—What's the Reason Behind the Shift?" *RedState*, November 12, 2020, https://redstate.com/bradslager/2020/11/12/fox-news-moves-left-and-their-new-pr-firm-is-only-part-of-the-reason-behind-the-shift-n278822

29   Selwyn Duke, "'Whatfinger News': What the Drudge Report Was Meant to Be," *New American*, 2018, https://thenewamerican.com/whatfinger-

news-what-the-drudge-report-was-meant-to-be/

30   Ryan Bomberger, "I Went to Wheaton to Talk Abortion. Student Govt. Denounced Me, Said Talk Made Some Feel 'Unsafe,'" *Life Site*, 2018, https://www.lifesitenews.com/opinion/i-went-to-wheaton-to-talk-abortion-the-student-govt-flipped-out

31   Kevin Williamson, "What's Wrong with the Audubon Society," *National Review*, 2021, https://web.archive.org/web/20210518112347/https://www.nationalreview.com/the-tuesday/whats-wrong-with-the-audubon-society/

32   "Rent-Seeking," n.d. Corporate Finance Institute, https://corporatefinanceinstitute.com/resources/knowledge/economics/rent-seeking/

33   Russ Choma, "Learning from Microsoft's Mistakes, Google Invests Heavily in Influence," OpenSecrets.org, January 2013, https://www.opensecrets.org/news/2013/01/learning-from-microsofts-mistakes-g/

34   Adolph Reed Jr., "Antiracism: A Neoliberal Alternative to a Left," *Dialectical Anthropology* 42, 2: 2018, pp. 105–115.

35   Debra Heine, "Poll: Americans Overwhelmingly Oppose Teaching Critical Race Theory in Schools," *Tennessee Star*, June 9, 2021, https://tennesseestar.com/2021/06/09/poll-americans-overwhelmingly-oppose-teaching-critical-race-theory-in-schools/

36   Robert Kraychik, "Exclusive—Sen. Josh Hawley: Break Up Big Tech Monopolies to Protect Free Market," *Breitbart*, May 7, 2021, https://www.breitbart.com/radio/2021/05/07/exclusive-sen-josh-hawley-break-up-big-tech-monopolies-to-protect-free-market/

37   Edmund Burke, "Reflections on the Revolution in France," 1789, Everyman's Library (1986).

38   Kevin Williamson, "Rotten Elites Give a Bad Name to 'Elitism,'" *National Review*, November 2015, https://www.nationalreview.com/2015/11/elitism-conservatives-anti-elitism.

39   Rosemary O'Leary, "Guerilla Employees: Should Managers Nurture, Tolerate, or Terminate Them?" *Public Administration Review*, 70(1), 2009, pp. 8–19, https://doi.org/10.1111/j.1540-6210.2009.02104.

40   David Mayhew, *Congress: The Electoral Connection*. New Haven, CT: Yale University Press, 1974.

41   Vivek Saxena, "Maher Slams 'Woke' Culture, Says it's Preventing America from Winning 'Battle for 21st Century' with China," *BizPacReview*, March 14, 2021, https://www.bizpacreview.com/2021/03/14/maher-slams-woke-culture-says-its-preventing-america-from-winning-battle-

for-21st-century-with-china-1042889/

42   The Editors of The National Review, "A Welcome Backlash against Criti-
        cal Race Theory," *National Review*, May 2021, https://www.national-
        review.com/2021/05/a-welcome-backlash-against-critical-race-theory/

43   "Republicans Must Take On 'Woke Corporations' if They Want to Defeat
        the Globalist American Empire," *Revolver*, April 2021, https://www.re-
        volver.news/2021/04/georgia-republicans-delta-coca-cola-woke-capital-
        voting-rights-fraud/; and Mary Margaret Olohan, "Arkansas Gov
        Continues to Deny Bowing to Corporate Pressure on Trans Surgeries for
        Minors Ban," *Daily Caller*, April 8, 2021,
        https://dailycaller.com/2021/04/08/arkansas-governor-hutchinson-
        tucker-carlson-corporate-pressure/

44   *Precinct Strategy*, https://precinctstrategy.com/

45   Among them Bari Weiss, John McWhorter, Sam Harris, Bret Weinstein,
        Gad Saad, Joe Rogan, Jonathan Haidt, Bill Maher, and Tim Poole. See,
        Bari Weiss, "Resignation Letter," *New York Times*, 2020,
        https://www.bariweiss.com/resignation-letter; John McWhorter, *The
        Elect: Neoracists Posing as Antiracists and their threat to a Progressive
        America*. Self-published, 2021,
        https://johnmcwhorter.substack.com/p/the-elect-neoracists-posing-as-
        antiracists; Critical Thoughts, *Sam Harris on the Cult of Wokeness*
        (Video), YouTube, October 17, 2020.
        https://www.youtube.com/watch?v=-XRU62fIsH0; *The Sun*, "Racism Has
        Been Redefined," *Bret Weinstein on Woke Science & How Humans Suc-
        ceed* [Video], September 11, 2020, YouTube.
        https://www.youtube.com/watch?v=k1YZkAdn3Ls; Gad Saad, *The Para-
        sitic Mind: How Infectious Ideas Are Killing Common Sense*. New York:
        Simon and Schuster, 2020; JRE Clips, *Joe Rogan: The Redefinition of Rac-
        ism* [Video], YouTube, January 7, 2019,
        https://www.youtube.com/watch?v=7j57204BDL4; *Bill Maher, New Rule:
        White Shame, Real Time with Bill Maher* (HBO) [Video]. YouTube, Sep-
        tember 28, 2019, https://www.youtube.com/watch?v=T0q2ZR4nBuE;
        Timcast IRL, *Anti-Racism Does NOT Mean Not Being Racist, It Means
        MORE Authoritarianism* [Video], YouTube, September 15, 2020,
        https://www.youtube.com/watch?v=4GGP12UPHdo.

46   Kevin Narizny, n.d. "The Flawed Foundations of Critical Race Theory,"
        Lehigh University, https://www.lehigh.edu/~ken207/

47   Josh Hammer, "The Coalition of the Un-Woke," *Newsweek*, 2021,
        https://www.newsweek.com/coalition-un-woke-opinion-1580601

48   Robby Soave, "'Silence Is Violence': D.C. Black Lives Matter Protesters
        Adopt Strategy of Intimidating Random White People," *Reason*, August

25, 2020, https://reason.com/2020/08/25/black-lives-matter-protesters-dc-silence-is-violence-white-people/

49   Beth Baumann, "Kaepernick Is Wanting the Rage Mob to Cancel the 4th of July," *Townhall*, July 4, 2020, https://townhall.com/tipsheet/bethbaumann/2020/07/04/kaepernick-4th-of-july-is-just-a-celebration-of-white-supremacy-n2571882

50   Christopher Rufo, "Disney Backs Down," 2021, Christopherrufo.com. https://christopherrufo.com/disney-backs-down/

51   Steve Turley, *The New Conservative's Survival Guide to Big Tech Censorship*. Self-published, 2020, https://censorship.turleytalks.com/survival-guide

52   Rod Dreher, *The Benedict Option: A Strategy for Christians in a Post-Christian Nation*. New York: Sentinel, 2017.

53   Dreher, "Millennials & The Parallel Polis," *American Conservative*, 2018, https://www.theamericanconservative.com/dreher/millennials-parallel-polis-vaclav-benda-benedict-option/

54   Tom Owens, "Classical, Christian Education: Higher SAT Scores Than All Other School Types 'Without Even Trying,'" Dominion Christian School, 2020, https://www.dominionschool.com/dominion-blog/classical-christian-education-higher-sat-scores-than-all-other-school-types-without-even-trying

55   Brian Almon, "Review: HBO's 'Exterminate All the Brutes' Is Riddled with Revisionist Marxist Falsehoods," *The National Pulse*, 2021, https://thenationalpulse.com/culture/exterminate-all-the-brutes-review/?fbclid=IwAR0lQ-2Y1DQIS4vrFJ0mKj_l2hYJheAgkrryY-HUbHsVRH5-K_By7DsJA6tU

56   Doha Madani, "Netflix Indicted in Texas over 'Lewd' Depiction of Children in 'Cuties,'" NBC News, 2020, https://www.nbcnews.com/pop-culture/pop-culture-news/netflix-indicted-texas-over-lewd-depiction-children-cuties-n1242304

57   Kyle Rankin, (Director, Producer). "Run Hide Fight," United States, 2020, https://www.dailywire.com/videos/run-hide-fight.

58   Andrew Klavan, *Another Kingdom*. Nashville: Turner Publishing, 2019.

59   Tim Pearce, "Gina Carano to Produce and Star in Upcoming Film for the Daily Wire," *Daily Wire*, 2021, https://www.dailywire.com/news/gina-carano-to-produce-and-star-in-upcoming-film-for-the-daily-wire

60   Associated Press, "Idaho Company to Block Facebook and Twitter for Censorship," *US News*, January 11, 2021, https://www.usnews.com/news/best-states/idaho/articles/2021-01-

11/idaho-company-to-block-facebook-and-twitter-for-censorship.

61   Saul D. Alinsky, *Rules for Radicals: A Pragmatic Primer for Realistic Radicals*. New York: Random House, 1971.

62   Alinsky, p. 128.

63   Molly McHugh, "'Learn to Code': The Meme Attacking Media," *The Ringer*, January 29, 2019, https://www.theringer.com/tech/2019/1/29/18201695/learn-to-code-twitter-abuse-buzzfeed-journalists

64   Will Rahn and Dan Patterson, "What Is the QAnon Conspiracy Theory?" CBSNews, 2021, https://www.cbsnews.com/news/what-is-the-qanon-conspiracy-theory/

65   Brian Flood, "Liberal Media Pushed QAnon as New 'Boogeyman,' Post-Trump Face of Republican Party," Fox News, 2021, https://www.fox-news.com/media/media-trying-make-qanon-face-gop-post-trump

66   Daniel Dale, "The Long Tail of Trump's Big Lie: 9 Ways It Continues to Affect American Politics," CNN, 2021, https://www.cnn.com/2021/05/23/politics/trump-big-lie-impact/index.html

67   Evan Palmer, "What Is Blue Anon? Urban Dictionary Restores Phrase for 'Left-Wing Conspiracy Theories," *Newsweek*, 2021, https://www.newsweek.com/blue-anon-urban-dictionary-left-wing-hoaxes-1574733

68   Chris Bell, "Why Has Twitter Banned 1500 Accounts and What Are NPCs?" BBC, 2018, https://www.bbc.com/news/blogs-trending-45888176

69   Saul D. Alinsky, *Rules for Radicals: A Pragmatic Primer for Realistic Radicals*. Random House, 1971, p. 128.

70   See, Molly McHugh, "'Learn to Code': The Meme Attacking Media," *The Ringer*, January 29, 2019, https://www.theringer.com/tech/2019/1/29/18201695/learn-to-code-twitter-abuse-buzzfeed-journalists; Chris Bell, "Why Has Twitter Banned 1500 accounts and What Are NPCs?" BBC, 2018, https://www.bbc.com/news/blogs-trending-45888176

71   Felix Salmon, "Media Trust Hits New Low," *Axios*, 2021, https://www.axios.com/media-trust-crisis-2bf0ec1c-00c0-4901-9069-e26b21c283a9.html

72   *The Post Millennial*, "Streisand Effect: #BlueAnon Becomes Top Trend on Twitter After Censorship of Meme Backfires," 2021, https://thepostmillennial.com/streisand-effect-blueanon-becomes-top-trend-on-twitter

73   "How White People See Themselves When They Post Anti-White Posts,"

Digital Image. *Sizzle*, June 10, 2021, https://onsizzle.com/i/how-white-people-see-themselves-when-they-post-anti-white-19490099

74   Emily Garber, "The White Savior Complex," *Contemporary Racism*, 2020, http://contemporaryracism.org/123261/the-white-savior-complex/

CHAPTER 8

1   Helen Pluckrose and James Lindsay, *Cynical Theories: How Activist Scholarship Made Everything about Race, Gender, and Identity—And Why This Harms Everybody*. Durham, NC: Pitchstone Publishing. https://cynical-theories.com/

2   Voddie T. Baucham, *Fault Lines: The Social Justice Movement and Evangelicalism's Looming Catastrophe*. Washington, DC: Salem Books, 2021, https://www.voddiebaucham.org/fault-lines/

3   Matthew Lohmeier, *Irresistible Revolution*. Self-published, 2020. https://www.irresistiblerevolutionbook.com/

4   Jonathan Butcher and Mike Gonzalez, "Critical Race Theory, the New Intolerance, and Its Grip on America," The Heritage Foundation, 2020, https://www.heritage.org/civil-rights/report/critical-race-theory-the-new-intolerance-and-its-grip-america

5   *New Discourses*, https://newdiscourses.com/

6   Christopher F. Rufo, https://christopherrufo.com/

7   *CRT Legislation Tracker*, https://christopherrufo.com/crt-tracker/

8   Sam Dorman, "Legal Coalition Forming to Stop Critical Race Theory Training Around the Country," Fox News, 2020, https://www.foxnews.com/politics/legal-coalition-critical-race-theory

9   Christopher F. Rufo, "Failure Factory," 2021, https://christopherrufo.com/failure-factory/

10   Susan Edelman and Selim Algar, "Fourth White DOE Executive Sues Over Racial Discrimination," *New York Post*, October 1, 2019, https://nypost.com/2019/10/01/fourth-white-doe-executive-sues-over-racial-discrimination/

11   Paul Sperry, "Elite K-8 School Teaches White Students They're Born Racist," *New York Post*, July 1, 2016, https://nypost.com/2016/07/01/elite-k-8-school-teaches-white-students-theyre-born-racist/

12   Mica Soellner, "Former Smith College Employee, Who Quit over 'Racially Hostile Environment,' Says Students Called Police on Her During Visit," *Washington Examiner*, 2021, https://www.msn.com/en-us/news/us/former-smith-college-employee-who-quit-over-racially-hos-

tile-environment-says-students-called-police-on-her-during-visit/ar-BB1goAbA

13   Christopher F. Rufo, "Nuclear Consequences," 2020, https://christopher-rufo.com/nuclear-consequences/

14   Jesse Singal, "A Professor Pushed Back Against 'White Fragility' Training. The College Investigated Her for 9 Months," *Reason*, April 5, 2021, https://reason.com/2021/04/05/a-professor-pushed-back-against-white-fragility-training-the-college-investigated-her-for-9-months/

15   Christopher F. Rufo, "The Wokest Place on Earth," https://christopher-rufo.com/the-wokest-place-on-earth/

16   "No Left Turn in Education," https://noleftturn.us/

17   Elsie Arntzen to Attorney General Austin Knudsen, May 12, 2021, http://opi.mt.gov/Portals/182/AG%20Request%20Letter.pdf?ver=2021-05-12-103653-953; 2021, Op. Att'y Gen. No. 2021-001.

18   Daniel Vock and Ross Williams, "Attempts to Ban Teaching on 'Critical Race Theory' Multiply Across the U.S.," Georgia Public Broadcasting. May 24, 2021, https://www.gpb.org/news/2021/05/24/attempts-ban-teaching-on-critical-race-theory-multiply-across-the-us

19   Lee Brown, "Opponents of 'Critical Race Theory' Win Texas School Board Election," *New York Post,* May 3, 2021, https://nypost.com/2021/05/03/opponents-of-critical-race-theory-win-texas-school-election/

20   *CRT Legislation Tracker*, https://christopherrufo.com/crt-tracker/

21   Tenn. Public Chapter No. 493, 2021, https://publications.tnsosfiles.com/acts/112/pub/pc0493.pdf

22   Okla. HB 1775, 2021, http://webserver1.lsb.state.ok.us/cf_pdf/2021-22%20ENR/hB/HB1775%20ENR.PDF

23   Iowa House File 802, 2021, http://webserver1.lsb.state.ok.us/cf_pdf/2021-22%20ENR/hB/HB1775%20ENR.PDF

24   Idaho HB 377, 2021, https://legislature.idaho.gov/wp-content/uploads/sessioninfo/2021/legislation/H0377.pdf

25   "Model School Board Legislation to Prohibit Critical Race Theory," *Citizens for Renewing America,* June 4, 2021, https://citizensrenewingamerica.com/issues/model-school-board-language-to-prohibit-critical-race-theory-2/

26   Hayley Tschetter, "Parents Protest Implementation of Critical Race Theory at School Board Meeting," *Tennessee Star,* May 28, 2021,

https://tennesseestar.com/2021/05/28/parents-protest-implementation-of-critical-race-theory-at-school-board-meeting/

27   Ashe Schow, "New York Times Wildly Distorts State Bills Banning Critical Race Theory, Claims Republicans Want to Stop Teaching Slavery and Racism," *Daily Wire*, 2021, https://www.dailywire.com/news/new-york-times-wildly-distorts-state-bills-banning-critical-race-theory-claims-republicans-want-to-stop-teaching-slavery-and-racism

28   Christopher F. Rufo, [@realchrisrufo]. "This Is a USSR-Level Lie. None of the Bills Prohibit Schools from Teaching about Slavery or Racism" [Tweet]. Twitter, May 23, 2021, https://twitter.com/realchrisrufo/status/1396464770614661123

29   "1776 Commission Report," https://1776-commission-report.com/

30   "1776 Unites," https://1776unites.com/

31   Jim McConnell, "School Board Chair: Critical Race Theory Isn't Part of CCPS Curriculum," *Chesterfield Observer*, 2021, https://www.chesterfieldobserver.com/articles/school-board-chair-critical-race-theory-isnt-part-of-ccps-curriculum/; Joy Overbeck, "How to Unwoke Your School Board," *Townhall*, June 1, 2021, https://townhall.com/columnists/joyoverbeck/2021/06/01/how-to-unwoke-your-school-board-n2590264

32   James Lindsay, "OnlySubs: How Wokeness Narrows Empathy," *New Discourses*, April 2021, https://newdiscourses.com/2021/04/onlysubs-how-wokeness-narrows-empathy/

33   Mark Devine, "Will Critical Race Theory Break the Baptist Church?" *American Spectator*, 2020, https://spectator.org/crt-baptist-church/

34   Southern Baptist Church, "On Critical Race Theory and Intersectionality," 2019, https://www.sbc.net/resource-library/resolutions/on-critical-race-theory-and-intersectionality/

35   Mary Miller, "Critical Race Theory Comes to Church and My Children's Catholic Schools," *The Catholic World Report*, November 18, 2020, https://www.catholicworldreport.com/2020/11/18/critical-race-theory-comes-to-church-and-my-childrens-catholic-schools/

36   "Memorandum No. M-20-34," September 2020, https://www.whitehouse.gov/wp-content/uploads/2020/09/M-20-34.pdf

37   Janita Kan, "Arkansas Bans Government from Teaching Critical Race Theory," We the People Convention, 2021, https://wethepeopleconvention.org/articles/Arkansas-Gov-CRT-Ban

38   Claremont Institute, *J. D. Vance Outlines the Strategy Needed to Fight Back Against Woke Capital* [Video], YouTube, 2021, https://www.youtube.com/watch?v=nQvzGF3pxCQ

39   Emily Jashinsky, "Why Capitalists Like Jack Dorsey Keep Bankrolling Anticapitalists Like Ibram X. Kendi," *The Federalist*, August 20, 2020, https://thefederalist.com/2020/08/20/why-capitalists-like-jack-dorsey-keep-bankrolling-anticapitalists-like-ibram-x-kendi/

40   Kara Frederick, "Steven Crowder Is Suing YouTube Over Vague Rules, but It's Not Just about Him," The Heritage Foundation, 2021, https://www.heritage.org/technology/commentary/steven-crowder-suing-youtube-over-vague-rules-its-not-just-about-him

41   Robby Soave, "Yes, You Can Get Kicked Off Twitter for Saying 'Learn To Code'—Even If It's Not Harassment," *Reason*, March 11, 2019, https://reason.com/2019/03/11/learn-to-code-twitter-harassment-ross/

42   Steven Nelson, "Twitter Says Shaun King's Threat to Name Kenosha Cops 'Not in Violation' of Rules," *New York Post*, August 26, 2020, https://nypost.com/2020/08/26/twitter-ok-with-shaun-kings-threat-to-dox-kenosha-cops/

43   Mary Kay Linge and John Levine, "Twitter Censoring Post's Hunter Biden Exposé Is 'Election Interference': GOP Leaders," *New York Post*, October 17, 2020, https://nypost.com/2020/10/17/twitter-censoring-posts-biden-expose-is-election-interference-gop/

44   Tom Parker, "Facebook Permanently Suspends Page of Virginia State Senator Amanda Chase," *Reclaim the Net*, 2021, https://reclaimthenet.org/facebook-suspends-state-senator-amanda-chase/

45   Hannah Denham, "These Are the Platforms that Have Banned Trump and His Allies," *Washington Post*, January 11, 2021, https://www.washingtonpost.com/technology/2021/01/11/trump-banned-social-media/

46   "Governor Ron DeSantis Signs Bill to Stop the Censorship of Floridians by Big Tech," Florida Governor's Office, May 24, 2021, https://www.flgov.com/2021/05/24/governor-ron-desantis-signs-bill-to-stop-the-censorship-of-floridians-by-big-tech/

47   Anthony Izaguirre, "GOP Pushes Bills to Allow Social Media 'Censorship' Lawsuits," ABC News, 2021, https://abcnews.go.com/Business/wireStory/gop-pushes-bills-social-media-censorship-lawsuits-76308087

48   NCSL 50-State Searchable Bill Tracking Databases, https://www.ncsl.org/research/telecommunications-and-information-technology/ncsl-50-state-searchable-bill-tracking-databases.aspx

49   Editors, *The National Law Review,* "Biden Administration Revokes Diversity Training Restrictions and Takes Further Actions to Address Diverse Groups, 2021, https://www.natlawreview.com/article/biden-administration-revokes-diversity-training-restrictions-and-takes-further, Vol. XI, No. 64

50   Unity Training Solutions, https://unitytrainingsolutions.com/

51   Susana Rinderle, "Want to End Racism? Training Doesn't Work. So What
        Does?" *Talent Management and HR*, 2020, https://www.tlnt.com/want-
        to-end-racism-training-doesnt-work-so-what-does/

        Frank Dobbin and Alexandra Kalev, "Why Doesn't Diversity Training
        Work? The Challenge for Industry and Academia," *Anthropology Now*,
        10:2, 2018, pp. 48–55, DOI: 10.1080/19428200.2018.1493182

        Frank Dobbin, Alexandra Kalev, and Erin Kelly, "Diversity Management
        in Corporate America," Sage Publications, 2007, https://journals.sage-
        pub.com/doi/pdf/10.1525/ctx.2007.6.4.21

52   Grace Daniel, "You Can Hold Your Ground Against Critical Theory," *The
        American Mind*, 2021, https://americanmind.org/features/life-after-can-
        cellation/you-can-hold-your-ground-against-critical-theory/

GLOSSARY

1   Stanley Kurtz, "'Action Civics' Replaces Citizenship with Partisanship,"
        The American Mind, January 1, 2021,
        https://americanmind.org/memo/action-civics-replaces-citizenship-
        with-partisanship/

2   Amy Curran and Scott Warren, "Partisan Takes Won't Define Non-parti-
        san Action Civics," *NonDoc*, January 13, 2020,
        https://nondoc.com/2020/01/13/nonpartisan-action-civics/

3   Thomas Lindsay and Lucy Meckler, "'Action Civics,' 'New Civics,' 'Civic
        Engagement,' and 'Project-Based Civics': Advances in Civic Education?"
        Texas Policy Foundation, September 1, 2020,
        https://www.texaspolicy.com/action-civicsnew-civics-civic-engagement-
        and-project-based-civics-advances-in-civic-education/

4   David Randall, "Making Citizens: How American Universities Teach
        Civics," National Association of Scholars, January 9, 2017,
        https://www.nas.org/reports/making-citizens-how-american-univer-
        sities-teach-civics

5   Legal Information Institute. n.d. "Affirmative Action," Cornell Law
        School, https://www.law.cornell.edu/wex/affirmative_action

6   James Lindsay, "Ally/Allyship," *New Discourses,* 2020, https://newdis-
        courses.com/tftw-ally-allyship/

7   Ibram X Kendi, *How to Be an Antiracist*. New York: Random House,
        2019, p. 9. Kindle Edition; Lindsay.

8   Oliver Traldi, "'Tactics' Are Not the Problem with Antifa," *National Review*,

September 2017, https://www.nationalreview.com/2017/09/antifa-violence-tactics-anger-politics-attacks-liberals-too/

9   Leslie Gornstein, "What Is Antifa? Is It a Group or an Idea, and What Do Supporters Want?" CBS News, 2021, https://www.cbsnews.com/news/what-is-antifa/; Ron Blitzer, "FBI Director Wray: 'Antifa Is a Real Thing,' FBI Has Cases Against People Identifying with Movement," Fox News, 2020, https://www.foxnews.com/politics/fbi-director-wray-antifa-cases-real

10 About. n.d. "Black Lives Matter," https://blacklivesmatter.com/about/

11 James Lindsay, "Black Lives Matter." *New Discourses,* 2020, https://newdiscourses.com/tftw-black-lives-matter/

12 Lindsay, "Black Lives Matter."

13 Black Nationalism (definition), https://www.lexico.com/en/definition/black_nationalism

14 The Editors of Encyclopaedia Britannica, n.d. "Black Nationalism." *Encyclopaedia Britannica,* https://www.britannica.com/event/black-nationalism

15 James Lindsay, "Cisgender," *New Discourses*, 2020, https://newdiscourses.com/tftw-cisgender/

16 "Civil Rights vs. Civil Liberties," *Find Law*, 2021, https://www.findlaw.com/civilrights/civil-rights-overview/civil-rights-vs-civil-liberties.html

17 "Civil Rights vs. Civil Liberties."

18 Robert Longley, "What Is Colonialism? Definition and Examples," *ThoughtCo*, 2021, https://www.thoughtco.com/colonialism-definition-and-examples-5112779

19 James Lindsay, "Decolonize / Decoloniality," *New Discourses*, 2020, https://newdiscourses.com/tftw-decolonize-decoloniality/

20 James Muldoon, "Academics: It's Time to Get Behind Decolonizing the Curriculum," *The Guardian*, 2019, https://www.theguardian.com/education/2019/mar/20/academics-its-time-to-get-behind-decolonising-the-curriculum

21 Patrik Jonsson, "Beyond a 'Colorblind' America, a New Ideal," *The Christian Science Monitor*, 2016, https://www.csmonitor.com/USA/Society/2016/0803/Beyond-a-colorblind-America-a-new-ideal

22 Ibram X. Kendi, *How to Be an Antiracist*, 2019.

23 Communism (definition), https://www.lexico.com/en/definition/com-

munism; Terence Ball, n.d. "Communism," *Encyclopaedia Britannica*, https://www.britannica.com/topic/communism

24   Richard Delgado and Jean Stefancic, *Critical Race Theory: An Introduction*. New York: NYU Press, 2017.

25   James Lindsay (panelist), "The State of Civics and Education—Dangers and Opportunities Ahead," Leadership Program of the Rockies, June 5, 2021, Colorado Springs, CO.

26   Tori DeAngelis, "In Search of Cultural Competence," *Monitor on Psychology* 46(3), 2015, p. 64, https://www.apa.org/monitor/2015/03/cultural-competence

27   George Farmer, "How Schools and Teachers Can Get Better at Cultural Competence," *Education Next*, 2020, https://www.educationnext.org/how-schools-teachers-can-get-better-cultural-competence/

28   Bill Berkowitz, "'Cultural Marxism' Catching on," Southern Poverty Law Center, https://www.splcenter.org/fighting-hate/intelligence-report/2003/cultural-marxism-catching

29   James Lindsay, "Cultural Marxism," *New Discourses*, 2020, https://new-discourses.com/tftw-cultural-marxism/

30   Jonathan Culler, *On Deconstruction*. Ithaca, NY: Cornell University Press, 2014.

31   James Lindsay, "Deconstruction," *New Discourses*, 2020, https://newdiscourses.com/tftw-deconstruction/

32   "What is Doxing—Definition and Explanation," n.d. Kaspersky, https://www.kaspersky.com/resource-center/definitions/what-is-doxing

33   Center for Public Education, "Educational Equity: What Does It Mean? How Do We Know When We Reach It?" National School Boards Association, 2016, https://www.nsba.org/-/media/NSBA/File/cpe-educational-equity-research-brief-january-2016.pdf

34   "Equality (Noun)." *Oxford Advanced American Dictionary* at OxfordLearnersDictionaries.com, June 13, 2021, www.oxfordlearnersdictionaries.com/us/definition/american_english/equality

35   James Lindsay, "Equality/Equal Opportunity (Ideology)," *New Discourses*, 2020, https://newdiscourses.com/tftw-equality-equal-opportunity-ideology/; "Equity vs. Equality: What's the Difference?" Milken Institute School of Public Health, 2020, https://onlinepublichealth.gwu.edu/resources/equity-vs-equality/

36   Equal opportunity (definition), https://www.merriam-webster.com/dictionary/equal%20opportunity

37   The Editors of Encyclopaedia Britannica, n.d. "Equal protection," *Encyclopaedia Britannica*, https://www.britannica.com/topic/equal-protection

38   James Lindsay, "Equity," *New Discourses*, 2020, https://newdiscourses.com/tftw-equity/; "Equity vs. Equality: What's the Difference?" Milken Institute School of Public Health, 2020, https://onlinepublichealth.gwu.edu/resources/equity-vs-equality/

39   James Lindsay, "Ethnomathematics," *New Discourses*, 2020, https://newdiscourses.com/tftw-ethnomathematics/

40   Richard Delgado and Jean Stefancic (Eds.), *Critical Race Theory: An Introduction* (3rd Ed.). New York: New York University Press, 2001, p. 147.

41   James Lindsay, "False Consciousness," *New Discourses*, 2020, https://newdiscourses.com/tftw-false-consciousness/

42   Cheryl Staats, "State of the Science: Implicit Bias Review 2013," Kirwan Institute, Ohio State University, 2013, https://kirwaninstitute.osu.edu/sites/default/files/2019-06/SOTS-Implicit_Bias.pdf; James Lindsay, "Implicit Bias," *New Discourses,* 2020 https://newdiscourses.com/tftw-implicit-bias/

43   James Lindsay, "Inclusion," *New Discourses,* 2020, https://newdiscourses.com/tftw-inclusion/

44   Kenton Bell (Ed.), "Interest Convergence," in *Open Education Sociology Dictionary*, 2014, https://sociologydictionary.org/interest-convergence/

45   James Lindsay, "Intersectionality," *New Discourses*, 2020, https://newdiscourses.com/tftw-intersectionality/

46   James Lindsay, "Marginalization," *New Discourses*, 2020, https://newdiscourses.com/tftw-marginalization/

47   Meritocracy (definition), https://www.merriam-webster.com/dictionary/meritocracy

48   James Lindsay, "Meritocracy (Ideology)," *New Discourses*, 2020, https://newdiscourses.com/tftw-meritocracy-ideology/

49   Metanarrative, n.d. *New World Encyclopedia*, https://www.newworldencyclopedia.org/entry/metanarrative

50   Jenée Desmond-Harris, "What Exactly Is a Microaggression?" *Vox*, February 16, 2015, https://www.vox.com/2015/2/16/8031073/what-are-microaggressions; Lindsay, James. 2020. "Microaggressions." *New Discourses,* https://newdiscourses.com/tftw-microaggressions/

51   James Lindsay, "Oppression," *New Discourses*, 2020, https://newdiscourses.com/tftw-oppression/

52   Robert Longley, "What is Political Correctness?" *ThoughtCo*, 2019,

https://www.thoughtco.com/what-is-political-correctness-4178215

53   "Politically correct," *Conservapedia*, 2021,
     https://www.conservapedia.com/Politically_correct

54   Brian Duignan, n.d. "Postmodernism," *Encyclopaedia Britannica*.
     https://www.britannica.com/topic/postmodernism-philosophy

55   Carlos Hoyt Jr., "The Pedagogy of the Meaning of Racism: Reconciling a
     Discordant Discourse," *Social Work* 57(3), 2012, pp. 225–234.

56   James Lindsay, "Privilege," *New Discourses*, 2020,
     https://newdiscourses.com/tftw-privilege/

57   Safe space (definition), https://www.lexico.com/en/definition/safe_space;
     Safe space, https://www.merriam-webster.com/dictionary/safe%20space

58   N'dea Yancey-Bragg, "What Is Systemic Racism? Here's What It Means
     and How You Can Help Dismantle It," *USA Today*, 2021,
     https://www.usatoday.com/story/news/nation/2020/06/15/systemic-rac-
     ism-what-does-mean/5343549002/

59   See James Lindsay, "Racism (Systemic)," *New Discourses*, 2020,
     https://newdiscourses.com/tftw-racism-systemic/

60   "Tolerance (Noun)," Merriam-Webster.com, June 13, 2021,
     https://www.merriam-webster.com/dictionary/tolerance

61   Bradley Campbell and Jason Manning, "The Rise of Victimhood Culture:
     Microaggressions, Safe Spaces, and the New Culture Wars," 2018. Lon-
     don: Palgrave Macmillan; Art Keller, "Critical Race Theory Is a Victim-
     ization Cult," *New Discourses*, 2020,
     https://newdiscourses.com/2020/06/critical-race-theory-victimization-
     cult/

62   Sandra Harding, *The Feminist Standpoint Theory Reader: Intellectual and
     Political Controversies*. New York: Routledge, 2004, pp. 7–8; James Lind-
     say, "Standpoint Epistemology," *New Discourses*, 2020, https://newdis-
     courses.com/tftw-standpoint-epistemology/

63   James Lindsay, "Ways of Knowing," *New Discourses*, 2020, https://new-
     discourses.com/tftw-ways-of-knowing/

64   Robin DiAngelo, "White Fragility," *International Journal of Critical Ped-
     agogy* 3(3), pp. 54–70, 2011

65   James Lindsay, "White Fragility," *New Discourses*, 2020, https://newdis-
     courses.com/tftw-white-fragility/

66   White nationalist (definition), https://www.merriam-webster.com/dic-
     tionary/white%20nationalist

67   Amanda Taub, "'White Nationalism' Explained," *New York Times*, No-

vember 22, 2016, https://www.nytimes.com/2016/11/22/world/ameri-cas/white-nationalism-explained.html; See also Carol M. Swain, *The New White Nationalism in America: Its Challenge to Integration*. Cambridge: Cambridge Press, 2002.

68   James Lindsay, "White Supremacy," *New Discourses,* 2020, https://new-discourses.com/tftw-white-supremacy/

69   Robin DiAngelo, *What Does It Mean to Be White?: Developing White Racial Literacy* (Revised Edition). Bern, Switzerland: Peter Lang, 2016, p. 148.

70   Özlem Sensoy and Robin DiAngelo, *Is Everyone Really Equal?: An Introduction to Key Concepts in Social Justice Education*, first edition. New York: Teachers College Press, 2012, p. 119; James Lindsay, "Whiteness," *New Discourses*, 2020, https://newdiscourses.com/tftw-whiteness/

71   James Lindsay, "Woke/Wokeness," *New Discourses*, 2020, https://newdiscourses.com/tftw-woke-wokeness/

APPENDIX A

Resources

COMBATTING CRT

1776 Unites, https://1776unites.com/our-work/curriculum/

Citizens for Renewing Democracy,
https://citizensrenewingamerica.com/issues/combatting-critical-race-theory-in-your-community/

For Kids and Country, https://www.forkidsandcountry.org/

Foundation Against Intolerance and Racism,
https://www.fairforall.org/about/

Let's Roll America, https://letsrollamerica.us/

No Left Turn in Education, https://noleftturn.us/

Parents Against Critical Theory, https://stoplcpscrt.com/about/

Parents Defending Education, https://defendinged.org/

Renew, https://renew.org/

Stand Against Racism and Radicalism in the Services,
https://www.starrs.us/

The American Principles Project, https://americanprinciplesproject.org/

Unity Training Solutions, https://unitytrainingsolutions.com/

US Parents Involved in Education, https://uspie.org/

CRT IN PRACTICE
(E.G., IN EDUCATION AND IN EMPLOYMENT)

Critical Race Training in Education

https://criticalrace.org/

Christopher Rufo

Articles: https://christopherrufo.com/

"CRT Legislation Tracker," https://christopherrufo.com/crt-tracker/

"Critical Race Theory Briefing Book," http://christopherrufo.com/crt-briefing-book/?mc_cid=340fbeafe6&mc_eid=da593a21b6

Manhattan Institute (event), "Parent-led Challenges to Critical Race Theory"

https://www.manhattan-institute.org/parent-led-challenge-critical-race-theory

Eagle Forum, https://eagleforum.org/topics/education/crt.html

CRT IN THEORY
From CRT critics
Online summaries

New Discourses

Home page, https://newdiscourses.com/

Social Justice Encyclopedia, https://newdiscourses.com/translations-from-the-wokish/

Neil Shenvi Apologetics, https://shenviapologetics.com/

Kevin Narizny, "The Flawed Foundations of Critical Race Theory"

https://www.lehigh.edu/~ken207/

Conservapedia, "Cultural Marxism,"

https://www.conservapedia.com/Cultural_Marxism

PragerU, "What Is Critical Race Theory?"

https://www.prageru.com/video/what-is-critical-race-theory/

PragerU, "Critical Race Theory: The Anti-Civil Rights Movement"

https://www.prageru.com/video/critical-race-theory-the-anti-civil-rights-
movement/

PragerU, "James Lindsay on Critical Race Theory: How Worried Should You Be?"

https://www.prageru.com/video/james-lindsay-on-critical-race-theory-
how-worried-should-you-be/

SOME IMPORTANT WORKS

Arnn, Larry, Carol Swain, and Matthew Spalding, eds., *The 1766 Report.* New York: Encounter Books, 2021

Baucham, Voddie, *Fault Lines: The Social Justice Movement and Evangelicalism's Looming Catastrophe.* Washington, DC: Salem Books, 2012.

Breitbart, Andrew, *Righteous Indignation: Excuse Me While I Save the World.* Hachette: UK, 2011.

Butcher, Jonathan, and Mike Gonzalez, "Critical Race Theory, the New Intolerance, and Its Grip on America." Heritage Foundation Backgrounder 3567: 2020–12.

Campbell, Bradley, and Jason Manning, T*he Rise of Victimhood Culture: Microaggressions, Safe Spaces, and the New Culture Wars.* London: Palgrave Macmillan, 2018.

Friedrichs, Rebecca, *Standing Up to Goliath: Battling State and National Teachers' Unions for the Heart and Soul of Our Kids and Country.* New York: Post Hill Press, 2018.

Kennedy, Duncan, "The Critique of Rights in Critical Legal Studies," *Left Legalism/Left Critique* 178: 216–227.

Lohmeier, Mathew, *Irresistible Revolution: Marxism's Goal of Conquest & the Unmaking of the American Military.* Self-published, 2021.

Pluckrose, Helen, and James Lindsay, *Cynical Theories: How Activist Scholarship Made Everything about Race, Gender, and Identity.* Durham, NC: Pitchstone, 2020.

Pyle, Jeffrey, "Race, Equality and the Rule of Law: Critical Race Theory's Attack on the Promises of Liberalism." *BCL* Rev 40, 3: 1998, pp. 787–827

FROM CRT PROPONENTS

Bell, Derrick:

"Brown v. Board of Education and the Interest-Convergence Dilemma." *Harvard Law Review 93*, 3: 1980, 518–533.

"Racial Realism." *Connecticut Law Review 24*, 2: 1992, 363–379.

"Who's Afraid of Critical Race Theory?" *University of Illinois Law Review*, 1995, pp. 893–910.

Bonilla-Silva, Eduardo, *Racism Without Racists: Color-blind Racism and the Persistence of Racial Inequality in the United States.* Maryland: Rowman & Littlefield Publishers, 2006.

Crenshaw, Kimberlé, "Mapping the Margins: Intersectionality, Identity Politics, and Violence against Women of Color," *Stanford Law Review 43*, 6: 1991, pp. 1241–1299.

Delgado, Richard and Jean Stefancic:

Must We Defend Nazis? Why the First Amendment Should Not Protect Hate Speech and White Supremacy. New York: NYU Press, 1997.

Critical Race Theory: An Introduction. New York: NYU Press, 2017.

DiAngelo, Robin, *White Fragility: Why It's So Hard for White People to Talk About Racism.* Boston: Beacon Press, 2018.

Harris, Angela., "The Jurisprudence of Reconstruction." *California Law Review 82*, 4: 1994, pp. 741–785.

Harris, Cheryl, "Whiteness as Property," *Harvard Law Review 106*, 8: 1993, pp. 1707–1791.

Hoyt, Carlos, "The Pedagogy of the Meaning of Racism: Reconciling a Discordant Discourse." *Social Work 57*, 3: 2012, pp. 225–234.

Kendi, Ibram X., *How to Be an Antiracist.* New York: One World, 2019.

Tate IV, William, "Chapter 4: Critical Race Theory and Education: History, Theory, and Implications." *Review of Research in Education 22*, 1: 1997, pp. 195–247.

SOME IMPORTANT RELATED WORK
(WHITENESS STUDIES)

Garvey, John and Noel Ignatiev, "Toward a New Abolitionism: A Race Traitor Manifesto," *Whiteness: A Critical Reader*: 1997, pp. 346–49.

Frankenberg, Ruth, *White Women, Race Matters: The Social Construction of Whiteness*. Minnesota: University of Minnesota, 1993.

McIntosh, Peggy, "White Privilege: Unpacking the Invisible Knapsack," *Peace and Freedom Magazine,* pp. 10–12, 1988.

Roediger, David, *Towards the Abolition of Whiteness: Essays on Race, Politics, and Working Class History.* New York: Verso, 1994.

Stowe, David, "Uncolored People: The Rise of Whiteness Studies," *Lingua Franca 6,* 6: 1996, pp. 68–77.

APPENDIX B

Model School Board Language to Prohibit Critical Race Theory

Source: "Model School Board Legislation to Prohibit Critical Race Theory," Citizens for Renewing America, June 4, 2021, https://citizensrenewingamerica.com/issues/model-school-board-language-to-prohibit-critical-race-theory-2/

Model School Board Language to Prohibit Critical Race Theory

Purpose

The purpose of this policy (or resolution) is to prohibit:
- the teaching and promotion of critical race theory,
- divisive concepts, and
- other forms of government-sanctioned or -facilitated racism in

our school district and to uphold the foundational American principle that all people are created equal and are endowed by their Creator with unalienable rights to life, liberty, and the pursuit of happiness.

Section 1. Definitions

A. *"Critical Race Theory"* means any theory or ideology that:

1. Derives or otherwise traces its origins or influences from, or pertinently overlaps with, the "Critical Theory" social philosophy espoused by the Frankfurt School;
2. Teaches or promotes that social problems are created by racist or patriarchal societal structures and systems;
3. Espouses the view that one race is inherently racist, sexist, or intentionally or inadvertently oppressive;
4. Espouses the view that one race is inherently responsible for the intentional or inadvertent oppression of another race;
5. One race or sex is superior to another race or sex;
6. A person should be discriminated against because of the race or sex attributed to them or be treated differently based on that classification;
7. A person's moral character is determined by the race or sex attributed to them;
8. The race or sex attributed to a person makes them responsible for past transgressions of that race or sex;
9. A person would feel discomfort, guilt, anguish, or any other form of psychological, physical, or any other kind of distress on account of the race or sex attributed to them; and
10. Work ethic or devotion to duty and obligations is inherently racist or sexist.

B. *"Divisive Concepts"* mean any concept that espouses:

1. One sex, race, ethnicity, color, or national origin is inherently superior to any other sex, race, ethnicity, color, or national origin;

2. The United States is fundamentally or systemically racist or sexist;

3. An individual, by virtue of the sex, race, ethnicity, religion, color, or national origin attributed to them is inherently racist, sexist, or otherwise prejudiced or oppressive, whether consciously or unconsciously;

4. An individual should be discriminated against or receive adverse treatment solely or partly because of the sex, race, ethnicity, religion, color, or national origin attributed to them;

5. An individual's moral character is necessarily determined by the sex, race, ethnicity, religion, color, or national origin attributed to them;

6. An individual, by virtue of the sex, race, ethnicity, religion, color, or national origin attributed to them, bears responsibility for actions committed in the past by other members of the same (or any other) sex, race, ethnicity, religion, color, or national origin;

7. Any individual should be targeted and made to feel discomfort, guilt, anguish, or any other form of psychological distress due to the sex, race, ethnicity, religion, color, or national origin attributed to them;

8. Meritocracy or traits such as a work ethic or devotion to duty and obligations are racist or sexist, or were created or recognized by a particular race to oppress another race; or

9. The term "divisive concept" includes any other form of race or sex stereotyping or any other form of race or sex scapegoating;

   (a) "Race or sex stereotyping" means ascribing character traits, values, moral and ethical codes, privileges, status, or beliefs to a race or sex, or to an individual because of his or her race or sex;

   (b) "Race or sex scapegoating" encompasses any claim

that, consciously or unconsciously, and by virtue of his or her race or sex, members of any race are inherently racist or are inherently inclined to oppress others, or that members of a sex are inherently sexist or inclined to oppress others.

C. *"Government-sanctioned or -facilitated racism"* means any concept, theory, ideology, action, omission, custom, policy or practice enacted by elected officials or taxpayer-funded entities that:

1. Supports, promotes, or affirms the adverse treatment of an individual by virtue of the race attributed to them;
2. Results in the affirmation, adoption, or adherence to viewpoints that treat individuals adversely by virtue of the race attributed to them;
3. Reinforces, supports, or affirms the ahistorical and racist ideas promoted by the 1619 Project and likeminded endeavors and organizations or otherwise derives or can trace its origins to the essays, curricula, and writings of the 1619 Project and similar endeavors.

Section 2. Prohibitions

A. The tenets outlined in section (1)(B), often found in "critical race theory," undermine a free society and sound education and otherwise exacerbate and inflame divisions on the basis of sex, race, ethnicity, religion, color, national origin, or other criteria in ways contrary to the unity of the nation, the founding principles of the nation, and the well-being of the citizens of [insert local school board jurisdiction].

B. Therefore, no school district, or public school, including a public charter school, shall direct or otherwise compel students to personally affirm, adopt, or adhere to any of the following tenets:

1. That any sex, race, ethnicity, color, or national origin is inherently superior or inferior;
2. That individuals should be discriminated against or receive adverse treatment solely or partly because of the sex, race, ethnicity, religion, color, or national origin attributed to them;

3. That an individual, by virtue of the sex, race, ethnicity, religion, color, or national origin attributed to them, are inherently responsible for actions committed in the past by other members of the same (or any other) sex, race, ethnicity, religion, color, or national origin;

4. That an individual, by virtue of the sex, race, ethnicity, religion, color, or national origin attributed to them is inherently racist, sexist, or oppressive, whether consciously or unconsciously;

5. That an individual's moral character is necessarily determined by the sex, race, ethnicity, religion, color, or national origin attributed to them;

6. That an individual should be targeted and made to feel discomfort, guilt, anguish, or any other form of psychological, physical, or any other kind(s) of distress due to the sex, race, ethnicity, religion, color, or national origin attributed to them;

7. That meritocracy or traits such as a hard work ethic are racist or sexist, or were created by a particular race to oppress another race; or

8. That the United States is fundamentally or systemically racist or sexist;

C. No distinction among or classification of students shall be made on account of race, color, or national origin.

D. No course of instruction, unit of study, or any other curricular or extracurricular offerings directing, facilitating, enabling, permitting, sponsoring, supporting or otherwise compelling students to personally affirm, adopt, or adhere to any of the tenets identified in paragraph (B) of this subsection shall be used or introduced in any school within the jurisdiction of this board of education. Nor shall students, directly or indirectly, be encouraged or incentivized in any manner to do so.

E. All training programs for school district employees relating to diversity, equity, or inclusion must adhere to the provisions outlined in section (2)(B) and shall, before being used, be reviewed by the board of education for full compliance with this subchapter. This review shall also be available for discussion in a public format to provide parents, guardians, and residents with a meaningful opportunity to participate, review, and provide input on any proposed guidelines relating to diversity, equity, or inclusion training for school district employees.

F. Notwithstanding any other provision of law, this section does not prohibit schools, or entities under the jurisdiction of the board of education, from including, as part of a course of instruction or in a curriculum or instructional program, or from allowing teachers or other employees to use supplemental instructional materials that include:

1. The history of an ethnic group, as described in textbooks and instructional materials adopted in accordance with approved curriculum;
2. The discussion of otherwise controversial aspects of history, only if done so without violating the provisions outlined in section (2)(B) and only if done so by presenting, from a holistic point of view, a complete, neutral, and unbiased perspective of the subject matter or prism;
3. The instruction on the historical oppression of a particular group of people based on race, ethnicity, class, nationality, religion, or geographic region; or
4. Primary source documents relevant to such a discussion if otherwise approved for use in curriculum or trainings, and otherwise comports with the provisions of above sections.

Section 3. Applicability to School Districts

Notwithstanding any other provision of law, the provisions outlined in section (2) shall also be applied to all employees at a covered school in the school district as outlined in section (2)(B).

A. A covered school shall not teach, instruct, or train any employee, contractor, staff member, administrator, supervisor, assistant, part-time employee, parent volunteer, or any other individual or group, to adopt, support, or promote critical race theory, divisive concepts, or government-sanctioned or -facilitated racism as defined by the provisions herein enacted.

B. No employee of the board of education shall face any direct or indirect adverse consequences, penalty or discrimination on account of his or her refusal to support, believe, endorse, embrace, confess, act upon, or otherwise assent to critical race theory, divisive concepts, or government-sanctioned or -facilitated racism as defined.

1. The fair and equal treatment of individuals is an inviolable principle that must be maintained in the state workplace.
2. The administrative head of each school shall use his or her authority to ensure that the school employees during work hours, and any contractors hired by the school to provide training, workshops, forums, or similar programming, for purposes of this section, to school employees do not teach, advocate, act upon, or promote in any training to school employees critical race theory, divisive concepts, or government-sanctioned or -facilitated racism as defined.

C. No funds shall be expended by the board of education, or any entity under the board of education's jurisdiction, for any purpose prohibited in section 2, section (3)(A), and section (3)(B).

Section 4. Penalties

Along with the board of education, the principal of each school subject to the provisions herein enacted must enforce those provisions. The principal may delegate some aspects of the responsibility of that enforcement so long as that principal remains active in the enforcement process. Notwithstanding any other provision of law, whenever a complaint concerning the potential violation of the provisions herein enacted by a covered school, school employee, or contractor is brought to the principal's attention or the principal has any cause to suspect that such a violation has occurred, is occurring, or may occur, the principal must notify the board of education in writing as expeditiously as is reasonable but within no later than 7 calendar days. The board of education then has 30 calendar days to complete an assessment of the covered school or school employee's violation and make it publicly available to residents within the school district.

A. If a covered school violates the provisions in section (2) or section

(3), the board of education, notwithstanding any other provision of state or federal law, shall sanction the school by providing public notice to residents within 30 calendar days, enacting a prohibition on participation in athletic competition, or otherwise bar the covered school from any participation in local or state academic or athletic activities for a period up to 30 days.

B. If a school employee violates the provisions in section (2) or section (3), the board of education, notwithstanding any other provision of state or federal law, shall require the school administrator to sanction the employee as follows:

1. Upon first offense, the employee shall be placed on 30 days of administrative leave without pay.
2. Upon second offense, the employee shall be terminated; and the school shall issue a public statement reiterating its commitment to upholding the fundamental American idea that all men are created equal and endowed by their Creator with unalienable rights to life, liberty, and the pursuit of happiness.

C. If a contractor provides a training for school employees relating to diversity, equity, or inclusion that teaches, advocates, or promotes critical race theory, divisive concepts, and government-sanctioned or -facilitated racism as defined, and such action is in violation of the applicable contract, the school entity that contracted for such training shall evaluate within 30 calendar days whether to pursue debarment of that contractor, consistent with applicable law and regulations.

1. If a contractor is found to be in violation of the applicable contract through the teaching or promotion of critical race theory, divisive concepts, or government-sanctioned or -facilitated racism as defined, then the contractor shall be debarred with public notice provided within 7 calendar days of the debarment of that contractor.

D. If a board of education member violates the provisions in section (2) or section (3) or otherwise lends material or any other tangible or intangible support, aid, assistance or encouragement to critical race theory, divisive concepts, or government-sanctioned or -facilitated racism as defined, the board of education, notwithstanding any other provision of state or federal law, shall notify the public within 7 calendar days and provide notice of a public forum to be held no later than 30 calendar days after notification.

1. The public forum shall be used to formally consider removal of the board of education member through a special election consistent with state and local election law and must provide parents, guardians, and residents with a meaningful opportunity to participate, review, and provide input on the consideration of removal of the board of education member.

Section 5. Additional Terms
Additional terms and concepts below that either wholly violate the above clauses, or which may if taught through the framework of any of the prohibited activities defined above, partially violate the above clauses in what is otherwise broadly defined as "critical race theory":

A. Critical Race Theory (CRT)
Action Civics
Social Emotional Learning (SEL)
Diversity, Equity, and Inclusion (DEI)
Culturally responsive teaching
Abolitionist teaching
Anti-racism
Anti-bias training
Anti-blackness
Anti-meritocracy
Obtuse meritocracy
Centering or de-centering
Collective guilt
Colorism
Conscious and unconscious bias
Critical ethnic studies
Critical pedagogy
Critical self-awareness
Critical self-reflection
Cultural appropriation/misappropriation

Cultural awareness
Cultural competence
Cultural proficiency
Cultural relevance
Cultural responsiveness
Culturally responsive practices
De-centering whiteness
Deconstruct knowledges
Diversity focused
Diversity training
Dominant discourses
Educational justice
Equitable
Equity
Examine "systems"
Free radical therapy
Free radical self/collective care
Hegemony
Identity deconstruction
Implicit/Explicit bias
Inclusivity education
Institutional bias
Institutional oppression
Internalized racial superiority
Internalized racism
Internalized white supremacy
Interrupting racism
Intersection
Intersectionality
Intersectional identities
Intersectional studies
Land acknowledgment
Marginalized identities
Marginalized/Minoritized/Under-represented communities
Microaggressions
Multiculturalism
Neo-segregation

Normativity
Oppressor vs. oppressed
Patriarchy
Protect vulnerable identities
Race essentialism
Racial healing
Racialized identity
Racial justice
Racial prejudice
Racial sensitivity training
Racial supremacy
Reflective exercises
Representation and inclusion
Restorative justice
Restorative practices
Social justice
Spirit murdering
Structural bias
Structural inequity
Structural racism
Systemic bias
Systemic oppression
Systemic racism
Systems of power and oppression
Unconscious bias
White fragility
White privilege
White social capital
White supremacy
Whiteness
Woke

Section 6. Non-Exhaustiveness of Section 5

The list of terms and concepts in section 5 is non-exhaustive. Section 5
applies to all terms or concepts that violate the provisions herein enacted.

Section 7. Usage of Sex or other Classifications Mentioned in this Enactment
The usage of sex or other related classifications mentioned in this enactment shall not be construed as an endorsement of deviations from biological sex. These classifications are intended to prevent, and shall have the effect of preventing, anyone from using any manner of fluidity or impermanence regarding sex to circumvent the purpose and objective of this enactment.

Index

About the Authors

Carol Swain is the host of the podcast *Be the People* and *Conversations with Dr. Carol Swain*. She is also the author or editor of ten books. Her work *Black Faces, Black Interests* has won three national awards, and her book *The New White Nationalism in America* was nominated for a Pulitzer Prize. Swain is a former professor of political science at Princeton and Vanderbilt Universities. Her opinion pieces have been featured in the *New York Times*, the *Washington Post,* the *Wall Street Journal,* and the *Epoch Times*. She holds a PhD from the University of North Carolina, Chapel Hill. She lives in Nashville, Tennessee.

Christopher Schorr joined the Marine Corps in 2003 and deployed to Iraq in 2005. Upon returning home, he served as a platoon sergeant in the Marine Corps Reserves and completed his BA in Political Science (summa cum laude) at the University of California, San Diego. Chris subsequently earned his doctorate in American Government at Georgetown University. His dissertation addresses the challenge posed by white nationalism to conservatism and to the American political system. He lives in Damascus, Maryland, with his wife, two small children, and one oversized dog.